How to Fail Successfully

WORKSHEETS

The worksheets in this book have
been designed to
facilitate review and
application of the
chapter material.
They can be used for Sunday school, campus situations, home
Bible-study groups, or adapted for individual devotions.

JILL BRISCOE

How To Fail SUCCESSFULLY

FLEMING H. REVELL COMPANY
OLD TAPPAN, NEW JERSEY

Unless otherwise indicated, Scripture quotations are from the King James Version of the Bible.

Scripture quotations identified NIV are from the Holy Bible, New International Version, copyright © 1978, New York International Bible Society. Used by permission.

Scripture quotations identified TLB are from The Living Bible, Copyright © 1971 by Tyndale House Publishers, Wheaton, Illinois 60187. All rights reserved.

The poem "Tears" is taken from FIGHT FOR THE FAMILY by Jill Briscoe. Copyright © 1981 by the Zondervan Corporation. Used by permission.

Library of Congress Cataloging in Publication Data
Briscoe, Jill.
   How to fail successfully.

   1. Failure (Christian theology)—Popular
works. 2. Briscoe, Jill. I. Title.
BT730.5.B74   248.   82-570
ISBN 0-8007-1303-6   AACR2

How to Fail Successfully

TO *Ruth*

my incredibly competent secretary, who has

Never Failed
to be a powerful prayer partner
a sweet support to my family
and most of all—
a friend!

Contents

Introduction

Jill Briscoe's *How to Fail Successfully* is not just another "how to" book. Rather, it deals with failure and what we do with it, as it is "all part of the process of being a Christian and goes on till the day you die."

God expects us to deal with our failures, though, and Jill has given many practical insights as proof of why failure is never final or doesn't have to be.

I was especially intrigued with the chapter "Blunt Believers" and Jill's treatment of the story from 2 Kings 6 about the axhead—the "iron did swim."

The chapter on "dry bones" is a must—a powerful message!

Written in Jill Briscoe's unique British style, much as she speaks, this book is warm, personal, and well worth the reader's time.

LEIGHTON FORD

It is hard to remember, when you're down physically and have blown it spiritually; when you are wiped out emotionally and feel ostracized socially, that

failure is never final.

Christians aren't *made*—they are in the making!

How to Fail Successfully

1

Shaggy Sheep

The Lord is my shepherd; I shall not want.

He maketh me to lie down in green pastures: he leadeth me beside the still waters.

He restoreth my soul: he leadeth me in the paths of righteousness for his name's sake.

Yea, though I walk through the valley of the shadow of death, I will fear no evil: for thou art with me; thy rod and thy staff they comfort me.

Thou preparest a table before me in the presence of mine enemies: thou anointest my head with oil; my cup runneth over.

Surely goodness and mercy shall follow me all the days of my life: and I will dwell in the house of the Lord for ever.

Psalm 23

*H*ow *do you follow the Shepherd, when you are being pushed around by the sheep?*

I didn't know I was a sheep in shepherd's clothing! My friends, if asked to describe me (and who needs enemies when they have friends like that?), would have said that I was a lively, arrogant, self-sufficient student, used to speaking with great authority from the depths of my considerable ignorance about nothing very much. Looking back, I don't know how I could have been so certain that I was qualified to shepherd others, and so blind to the fact that I was actually being led from behind. One of the problems about being led from behind, however, was that none of my friends had any sense of direction either. We all lived for the present moment with little or no sense of destiny, letting the world go by.

Have you ever driven down a narrow road behind a bunch of sheep? At the approach of the car, the animals at the back panic, and quicken their pace, so that the leaders are propelled forward, despite themselves. This was what was happening to me. Pressured by that rear rush, I found myself the "up front" animal, crowded into behavior patterns by the pacesetters at my back. There seemed to be no other option but to explore the senseless, futile pursuits that lay along the crooked paths we took together. And yet, the first time another sheep tried to get me to admit my "sheepishness," I heartily resented the very idea. After all, I felt I had not had too much trouble doing my own thing: being the one apple in a barrel full of oranges; wearing the slightly zany piece of clothing; catching the eye; drawing attention to myself. Therefore, I was understandably offended at the mere suggestion that I was being led meekly along.

It was during the second semester at college that I met the "lamb" who drew attention to my predicament. Something in my stomach had begun to hurt me painfully enough to cause the authorities to rush me into the hospital, and there I met Janet, who was placidly lying in the "stall" next to me.

As we had time on our hands, we were able to get to know each other, and it didn't take me long to realize that we were very different! She was somehow fresh, while I was somehow stale. She still had a song to sing, while I was well and truly sung out. She was kind and generous in her remarks about the people who were caring for her, while I was cruel and critical. Hearing her bleat appreciation all over the place only served to evoke a strange embarrassment in me. I did not know the verse of Scripture that said:

> Come now, and let us reason together, saith the Lord: though your sins be as scarlet, they shall be as white as snow; though they be red like crimson, they shall be as wool.

> Isaiah 1:18

However, already that inner debate had begun. I was responding internally about this strange difference I sensed in my new friend, and the guilt her transparent life evoked in me. Starting to face up to the divine queries concerning my crimson conscience that had been successfully chloroformed for so long, I turned to Janet for answers. Seeing my confusion, she shared the secret of her serenity with me. She had a Shepherd. He led her, fed her, and blessed her out of her socks (or hooves—if you'd prefer!). She told me that the Lord Jesus was her Shepherd and invited me to join His flock, so He could be my Shepherd, too. I asked her if she meant I should join a church, and if God happened to be a Methodist (as I had had that distinct impression when once I had attended a service in a fellowship of that denomination). She smiled and told me that there was only One Shepherd and one fold, even though His sheep met in various groups and locations under differing names. But the sheep that belonged to the One True Shepherd knew Him intimately and rec-

ognized others that knew Him as well. She showed me a verse in the
Bible that said:

All we like sheep have gone astray; we have turned every one to his
own way; and the Lord hath laid on him the iniquity of us all.

Isaiah 53:6

Then she explained the meaning, saying that our "own way" was
not God's way. She went on to relate that the Divine Shepherd had
sent His Son as a sacrificial lamb, and He had become our Substitute,
bearing the crimson deeds of the whole herd of the entire inhabited
earth. Deeply moved, I somehow knew in my heart that what she
was telling me was not fable, but fantastic fact; and bowing my
head in prayer, asked the Chief Shepherd to place me on His strong
shoulders and bring me home.

It was then that it all began. This grand adventure, this laughing
life, this earnest imperfect attempt to stumble on my way behind
my Unseen Guide. To put it another way: after eighteen years of
hollowship, I began a life of *followship*. I could now clearly see how I
had been a sheep in shepherd's clothing, and humbly acknowledging my sheepish nature, I bathed in His forgiveness, and had my
wool washed white.

The time had come to follow the Shepherd, instead of being
pushed around by the sheep, but very soon I realized that it is a lot
easier to be led from behind than in front. It had been compara-
tively easy to flow with the flow, but it was another ball game altogether to turn around and try to trot against the herd. I found out
that one was likely to end up with little hoof marks all over one's
cute freshly washed hide. It was not going to be as easy as I had
thought. The possibility even occurred to me that I might fail.
Fail to follow? screamed my inflated ego: *Impossible!* But the
more I tried to stay up with the Shepherd, the more I realized my
limitations and the more I had to admit my intrinsic sheepishness.
For example, there was a little matter of my friends. I had very few
of them, as I had had a nasty habit of trying to steal their dates,

and, as you can imagine, that didn't make for good, steady companionship.

When I became a Christian, I was down to one good friend and a couple of questionable ones, and it didn't take them long to realize I had stopped skipping merrily around the forbidden pastures we had grazed together. The first test came very shortly after I had given my life to Christ. An invitation arrived for all of us to attend a somewhat dubious party. CLOTHES OPTIONAL it read in small print at the bottom. My friends giggled and pointed the words out to me. I knew the Shepherd was not amused, but all the sheep were baaing their heads off, and all that was within me wanted to follow suit.

Surely it wouldn't matter if I just gave a fleet bleat, and then just didn't go to the party, I thought. That way I wouldn't make my friends mad by a "pious" response! "Come on, Jill," my best friend teased, poking me in the ribs. "Let's go! It will be fun, and we can always leave if it gets too bad!" Who was I going to follow? The choice was mine. With a mighty effort, I mumbled an excuse and lunged out of the room, acutely aware of the puzzled, whispered remarks that followed me. I felt miserable because I knew the parting of the ways had come for us, and yet I sensed the cool hand of the Shepherd on my head, approving my decision. I had passed the first test. I had followed the Shepherd.

The following day, flushed with success, and with my head held high, I dared the devil to take me on! I was quite sure that from that moment on the Shepherd would find me faithful. I had not yet discovered that failure (and what you do with it) is all part of the process of being a Christian, and goes on till the day you die! That very day I heard myself using language that should not have come out of the mouth of a saved sheep. The Book of Rules had told me I must "not take the name of the Lord in vain," and I knew I had failed to follow instructions. I remember being grievously disappointed in myself, and then feeling—literally—sick to my stomach, as I wondered if it was all over. Perhaps I had not really been converted in the first place. How could I have behaved in such a way if I was really born again? Seeking counsel from Janet, she explained that there was only *one* sheep that had ever followed the rules fully and faithfully—and that was Jesus. There had not been another one like Him since! She told me gently that my propensity to wander from the straight path had not surprised God at all. He was certainly the God of surprises but was never surprised Himself, she said. To be surprised would mean He didn't know everything, and since God was omniscient, He could never be shocked. He expected us to fail, she told me quietly. Seeing my startled expression, she added quickly, "But He expects us to deal with failure too! It's like a baby learning to walk. You expect the little thing to fall flat on his face, but you don't expect him to stay there. God has provided a precious personal power to deal with our weakness and waywardness. It is Jesus who will show us *how to fail successfully.*"

Over the years, I have come to realize that too many of God's people are afraid to fail. That is one of the reasons they do very little in the church. They reckon that the less they do, the less chance they will have to fail doing it. They dare not start in case they cannot finish. Or they want to do things "goodly" right away, so are not willing to start by doing them badly! Or then again they might have made a valid and valiant attempt to achieve, and failure has happened, with a resulting sense of shame and disillusionment that forbids another attempt.

When Stuart and I came to pastor a church in the USA, I honestly wanted to be the best pastor's wife that there had ever been. Having served all our missionary career with a parachurch organization, I had no idea what was involved. I had never been part of a church body as such. Discovering the expectations of our parishioners, I was driven to the rapid conclusion that I didn't have the gifts of ministry that were needed for the task at hand—and therefore failure was inevitable. Wanting to do the *best* job, I was not willing to do *the worst,* and wondered how God would remove me from the scene, so He could get on with His work. A bolt of lightning, perhaps, as I was hanging out the clothes? A quick accident on the freeway? That would be very easy to arrange, as everyone drove on the wrong side of the road (being from Britain, I was the only one driving on the right side!). *If I could just practice in private,* I thought miserably. Oh, to be invisible. If only I didn't have to be caught center stage, struck with evident stage fright every time I appeared in public!

It was Stuart that encouraged me to have a go even if I failed. "If a job's worth doing, it's worth doing badly," he remarked cheerfully.

"No, no," I muttered desperately. "You've got that all wrong. If a job's worth doing, it's worth doing well—and that's the problem. I can't do it well, so it's far better that I don't do it at all."

"Nonsense," he said. "It's better to do it badly than not do it at all!"

Searching through the Scriptures, the Shepherd encouraged me to try anyway:

> And whatsoever ye do, do it heartily, as to the Lord, and not unto men.
>
> Colossians 3:23

Well, I thought, *any old sheep can do that,* so *I'll do it heartily and badly!* I could at least fail forcefully. And so twelve years ago I began to do the things a pastor's wife is expected to do, heartily and badly. I failed and failed and failed again—and am still failing today; but here and there, I succeeded; discovering gifts I didn't know I had. After a while I even found myself doing some things "goodly" and the other things that I continued to do badly attracted so much attention (you can usually bank on that!) that some people watching me were greatly encouraged. They had been sitting in church for years—nothing more than pew warmers—because they had been afraid to fail. Watching me fail so heartily helped them to realize that even they could do a better job than that, and up they got off their evangelical beds of ease and helped me out.

Not only is this the way to get all the things that need doing done in the church, it's the way to demonstrate that obedience to the Shepherd's call is so important. I found out that pride lay behind most of my stubborn refusals to try—conceit that wouldn't be seen learning or appearing to be less than perfect. Once the sheep has shed the shepherd's clothing, it really doesn't mind the flock's seeing it is only a sheep—prone to wander, prone to fail—prone *period!*

As Robert Robinson's hymn succinctly puts it:

> Prone to wander, Lord, I feel it,
> Prone to leave the God I love.

Sheep fail. They fail to follow. Some go on failing all of their lives, until they wag their fuzzy little tails for the very last time. Someone needs to tell them that sheep have to learn to follow, and in the learning, they *will* fail. We also need to understand our wandering nature is never eradicated, just because we have joined the flock. It is because God knows us so well that He calls Himself our Shepherd. Not only has the Shepherd provided us with Christ's nature to counteract our selfish natures, He has laid down certain principles of "followship" for us. We can find them in the Twenty-third Psalm. Anyone who can read can read them there. But to read them is not to *do* them. To know that I must follow doesn't necessarily mean I will be found following. But, oh, how happy and contented I shall be if only I do!

I shall not want is not an idle promise. The Shepherd who offers us real happiness has the power to make that happen. At one time, Stuart and I were working hard with a youth mission in Europe, and badly needed a break. In those days, a holiday was a luxury we could not really afford. And so when Stuart promised he would take our family to Spain for two weeks, I didn't pay much attention to him. I knew he was willing, but I also knew very well that he was not financially able. A few days later, a wealthy friend offered to take us all along with him on a fantastic trip to the seaside. Immediately I started to pack, for I knew that our well-to-do mentor was not only willing, but had the resources to come through with his word. When the Divine Shepherd assures us that it will be worth our while to come along with Him—wherever He wants to lead us—we can know that He is not only willing, He is also able to make it the most satisfying experience of our lives! It is because *the Lord* who is the Great Provider is our Shepherd that we shall not want.

What is this grand provision we read about? He tells us that if we follow Him, we shall lie down and rest beside the still waters, and we shall eat in green pastures. What more could a tired, hungry, and thirsty animal need? Following Him, you will find yourself satisfied and edified. The Good Shepherd knows where food fit for a sheep is to be found. He knows that sheep dislike fish and chips, hamburgers and french fries, and so provides only the most suitable fare. When He tells us we shall "lie down" in green pastures, He knows that a sheep never lies down unless its stomach is full, and if we will fill our stomachs with His Word, we will not want to be skipping off looking for greener grass on the other side of the fence. Instead, we shall find ourselves content to settle down at His feet and enjoy His provision. He wants to see us lying flat on our little woolly backs, kicking our hooves around in the air, saying, "Oh, Shepherd, we really can't eat one more blade!"

Do we know, in reality, that plenty to eat and plenty to drink brings plenty of happiness? But, as the saying goes, you can take a sheep to the water but you can't *make* it drink! Quite so! The Shepherd does not grasp the sheep's mouth between His hands and chomp its jaws up and down. He leads the animals to the food, but the sheep have to eat it themselves. Likewise He doesn't sit on the sheep's back to force it to rest beside the still waters; the sheep has to bend its own knees! Most of us know where to open the Bible, where to start reading, and we know very well how to pray. But to know it is not to do it! On the other hand, some of us may not know how to get into the green pastures. For us it may not be a matter of willfully refusing to eat, but rather ignorance as to method or material, and we find ourselves needing some help in the matter.

I remember gazing at the new shiny Bible that Janet had just given me. Before meeting Janet, it had never occurred to me people read Bibles anywhere other than in church (and then only on Sundays of course). It had blown my mind to see Janet reading hers on a *Friday.* But where was I to start? Opening it at random, I read the word *Epistle. What was that,* I wondered? Reading down the page, I came across a similar-sounding word—*Apostle.* I wondered if an Apostle was the wife of an Epistle! I didn't know where to begin, and I didn't know where to end—I didn't understand it. In the words of an Ethiopian eunuch I was yet to meet:

How could I, except some man should guide me? . . .

See Acts 8:31

Maybe I was starting in the wrong place. Perhaps, like any other book, I should start at the front!

Janet (my undershepherd), seeing my predicament, explained that contrary to the way we read all other books, it was *not* a good idea to start at the beginning of the Bible. "The Scriptures are a library of many books," she said, "and you don't go into a public library and start at the door and work your way around. A fine place to start is an epistle, which is just an old-fashioned word for a *letter* that Paul wrote to 'new sheep' who had just joined the Shepherd's fold. He wrote these letters to help explain the way the sheep should walk in straight paths."

Janet helped me to read Philippians, and showed me how to underline God's instructions with certain colors. "Note His warnings with one, His commands with another, and His promises with another," she said. "Then underline the verse you like best, and write in the margin why you like it. After you have done all that, go out into the day and make a point of following the advice you have found." She advised me to keep a notebook to remind me of all that I had learned, and told me that as I began to do this, I would find myself grazing gratefully.

It is in the Word of God that we have right paths illuminated for us. His Word will be a light to our feet and a lamp to our path, and we need never worry that we might not know which path to take. If we are openly and honestly following along in His Word, He will make it clear enough! For example, He tells us to be good parents to our kids, and each of us to be faithful and spouse-supportive. We don't have to debate whether all those sorts of things are the right paths or not. They are very clearly signposted for us. All we have to do is follow.

But what if I fail to follow? Will He beat me with His rod, stick me with His staff, harass my conscience with bad dreams and hound me back to His side? No, He won't. He leads me. The difference between an eastern and western shepherd is interesting. A western shepherd "drives" his sheep, while an eastern shepherd "leads" them! God is an Eastern Shepherd! This does not mean that if we fail to follow He will note the fact, shrug His shoulders, and go whistling on His way, caring only for those who stay close to His side. We will see in a little while that He will use His rod and His staff when it is absolutely necessary for the survival of the sheep, but it does mean that *following* is our frightening free choice. He wishes it that way—He gives us the dignity of choosing whether we will fill our bellies with poison weeds or good grass. He will not violate our free will. He does, however, put pressure of another kind upon us that will help to keep us freely following Him. He lets us know in no uncertain terms that we will not be the only ones to get hurt if we fail! Not only could we lead other sheep into trouble, which is bad enough in itself—but He will suffer, too.

You see, He leads us in the paths of righteousness *for His name's sake.* If we really blow it, and people know we are professing Christians, our good name will undoubtedly suffer—but more importantly, so will His. Maybe we don't really care what people think of us—but if we care anything about God, we should worry just a little bit about our actions and what they are doing to *His* reputation! "But He isn't doing anything—I am!" you object. The problem is once you have joined His flock, you are identified with Him, and He is identified with you. People know that you belong to the fold, and the fact is that a shepherd is judged by his sheep. If you fail, people think God has failed, and we should all care a little bit about that.

I remember standing at the gate to the entrance of Jerusalem, watching the sheep come home. One man's flock was fat and satisfied. Another's came trotting along, and some of those sheep were shaggy and lean. One even had an ear bitten off. I couldn't help judging the shepherd by his scraggy sheep! In the spiritual realm, people judge the Shepherd by the sheep, too, and so we need to walk in right paths *for His name's sake.*

I asked a young boy once why he didn't go to church. "I don't go," he answered, "because once I went to watch the churchgoers. I sat outside the church and saw them all go in. An hour later they all came out. They looked exactly the same as they had when they all went in, so I reckoned that what they had been listening to in there hadn't made any difference, so there was no point in me wasting my time." The young man was judging the Shepherd by the sheep— what a shame!

You see, God made us originally like Himself, and when the human race fell into willful disobedience, we all lost something. We lost the clear-cut lines of the original image of God's character stamped on our spiritual features. We lost the desire to glorify Him. God wants to restore that original image in our lives. He wants us to be like Him again, and so He lends us His power to follow the right paths—and He even goes before us to show us the way. As we live "rightly," others will see Him in our behavior, and He will be glorified.

My mother loves antiques. She was always busy restoring some old chunk of wood—or so it appeared to us. But when her work was finished, the image that had been hidden emerged, bringing forth admiration and praise. *To fail successfully* means to decide that He must be allowed to complete His restoring work in our lives *for His name's sake;* to fail to follow, and to try, try again, until we find ourselves succeeding means that, in the end, our lives will give praise and appreciation to Him. After all, the whole duty of man is to bring glory to God.

"But what if I miss the path?" someone asks. "What if I marry the wrong man, or make a stúpid career decision, or simply sin because I want to go my own way more than I want to please God?"

Part of the secret of making sure you find the right path, and stay on it, is the establishing of good habits. Now that sounds pretty simple. A habit is something you do over and over again, until it becomes perfectly natural, and you don't even think about it any- more. As the eastern shepherd brought his sheep back to the fold each night, he would stand at the door and count each one. As he did so, he would put his hand on the head of the animal. He would make a habit of touching them all. If a careless shepherd neglected to habitually touch his sheep, they would soon cease to turn their heads when they heard his voice! This could be very serious when they were out on the hills, for if the habit had been broken, a warning shout from the shepherd would be ignored, and disaster could result.

If we make a habit of grazing in the green pastures and resting beside the still waters, and if we are experiencing His daily touch at the end of our day, then we will recognize His voice when He warns us of impending danger, and will not end up in a hole! Many of us are following so far behind our Shepherd that we scarcely believe in the presence of an enemy. This is another reason many of us fail. If we have not been practicing the presence of God, then we have probably been practicing the presence of our enemy, and he has been whispering in our ears that he does not exist! There *is* one who does not intend us to fail successfully, but desires instead to bury us under guilt and despondency, and wishes us to believe we need never know victory at all. If we practice *his* presence, we shall come to accept his premise that failure is normal and must be accepted. He lurks in the shadows and the valleys that we must all walk through while we are here on earth. He does indeed exist—and for one purpose: to make us fail. Just as God is the Author of all things alive and living, the enemy is the author of all things dead and dying. He lives in the darkness and plays on our fears and our failures. But we can learn to stick close to our Shepherd and need not fear that we must fail forever. We can say to Satan, "I will not listen to you; I will heed my Shepherd."

> Yea, though I walk through the valley of the shadow of death, I will fear no evil: for thou art with me; thy rod and thy staff they comfort me.
>
> Psalms 23:4

The devil knows that fear can cause us to fail to follow the Shepherd, whether it be the fear of death, or even the fear of failure. He knows that if he can frighten us from the Shepherd, he can get hold of us and gobble us up with fear. It was not until I recognized the fact that inordinate fear is a lack of trust—and a lack of trust is sin—that I was able to let Christ deal with it. The Bible tells me:

> . . . whatsoever is not of faith is sin.

Romans 14:23

And so I know to fail in faith is a grievous thing; indeed it hurts my Shepherd deeply. The fear of habitual failure in the Christian life can cause distance between God and me. The devil would have me suffer guilt, even before I am guilty! I must learn not to practice the presence of my enemy but rather to practice the presence of my God. This is where the secret lies: *for thou art with me.* The Bible does not only promise me the mountaintop but warns me of the valleys. The same Bible assures me I shall never be alone in those deep, dark places. My Shepherd will lead me through them, and while He is with me there, the shadows will flee away. When you practice the Shepherd's presence, your fears become like shadows, and you find it is never completely dark. For where there is shadow, there is always light! The light of His presence will bring luminous possibilities into sight, and you will be able to see your way out.

There are too many sheep who expect that the Shepherd will keep them safe and sound by keeping them shut up in the fold forever. That promise is for heaven alone, and nowhere in the Bible do I read that that will be the case on earth. John tells us that while we are here on earth the Good Shepherd will lead His sheep *out.* Then at the end of a day, He will lead them back *in.* In and out, in and out! *In* to remind them of their relationship with Him, and *out* to remake them, as they walk the lonesome valley, close to His side. It's *out* among the wolves of fear and the bears of doubt and the lions of adverse circumstances that the sheep learn to follow hard on the Shepherd's heels. They do not learn that in the safety of the fold. The fold is for fellowship and touching, for rest and restoration—the field is for practicing the pursuit of God.

When I first became a Christian, I enjoyed the fold fellowship so much, it was quite a shock to hear my Shepherd say, "Follow Me," and understand He wanted to lead me *out* into the cold world. It was hard to read the verse that said, "Behold, I send you forth as sheep in the midst of wolves!" (Matthew 10:16). But if He had not taught me that, I would have learned only to follow other sheep and not to follow the Shepherd at all. Some Christians never get out into the real world, and mistaking separation for isolation, are in danger of knowing only Christians' help and not Christ's. It is so comfortable to stay snugly in the fold, baaing sheep hymns and rubbing our white-washed wool up against a brother or sister sheep. But fold fellowship is not the only thing the Shepherd has in mind for us. If we are never out of the fold on "risk's edge," we shall never know His grand protection, His enabling, and His sharp reality when we need Him most. Some folk believe that a Good Shepherd will not allow any harm to come to His flock. The Divine Shepherd promises eventual eternal safety from all of our enemies, but He allows close contact with the lion, bear, or wolf on earth, in order to drive us to His side. Sometimes we cannot escape a scratch, a bite, or worse.

Often a rebellious and stupid sheep insists on going its own way so consistently that the Shepherd has no alternative but to chasten it a little for its own good. He loves the one He chastens, just as a father loves (and therefore chastens) his son. This is where the rod and staff come in. An eastern shepherd will take his rod and break a wayward lamb's leg with it; then he will carry the little thing next to his heart, until the leg heals. By the time the animal is put down on the ground, it has enjoyed such oneness with the shepherd that he never shows much inclination to stray again!

In the past, my Shepherd has broken my leg with many rods many times, not the least, the rod of loneliness. My husband traveled for months on end, and this gave me the chance to be held close to the heart of God. I surely followed hard on His heels after that experience!

A friend stopped in to see me this week. She surprised me with her visit and asked me what I was doing. I told her I was writing a book called *How to Fail Successfully.* She laughed at the title and then said, "If you want any tips give me a call. I'm 'between failures' at the moment, and life is good, but I've felt the heartbeat of God in the last few months—He has been *that* close to me!" Turning to go, she added, "If all that blessing can come out of an experience of failure, then I'm ready to fail again." I knew she had lost her husband, and had fallen apart for a few weeks. She felt she had failed to give a testimony during her grief. Lying in His arms, with her leg broken with the rod of bereavement, she experienced the love of God in her valley of death, and stopped blaming herself for her lack of faith. "He wanted to teach me to lie still until I was healed," she said. "What a relief to realize He didn't expect me to do anything else but rest. He's carried me right through that whole adjustment period, and here I am on the slopes again." I noticed she didn't say mountaintop—for who ever is found on the mountaintop when half of you has been taken away? But I watched her on the slopes feasting with God and I worshiped.

It is in the very presence of our archenemy, Satan himself, and his host of hellish helpers that we can sit down unafraid and unashamed and feast after failure. The devil will try and tell us we have failed once too often, and all we deserve is bread and water for the rest of our lives, but the Good Shepherd bids us to come to His feast. It is a feast of forgiveness. The best way to handle failure is to know that it is forgivable. I need never fear the anger of my Shepherd if I ask to try again. I will find only His loving arms, tender touch, and feast after all my failure.

It is at this feast that our Heavenly Shepherd will anoint our head with oil. There were three kinds of people anointed with oil in Old Testament times: prophets, priests, and kings. All needed a special unction from above to be able to carry out their huge responsibilities. Oil speaks of the Holy Spirit and also of joy. It is after a time of weakness and failure that we must return to Him and admit our own puny efforts have been pitifully futile. We need to ask humbly for His forgiveness and claim a special anointing for the task He has given us to do.

I have been given many an opportunity to speak. There are few things that frighten me more than sitting on a platform looking out at a sea of expectant faces, waiting for me to get up and say something relevant. Often I feel slightly stupid and a little bit ridiculous. "Deliver me," I pray, with my heart pounding, "from the art of 'almost' saying something!" If it were not for my conviction that the Shepherd has led me into that particular situation, I would not have the confidence that He would lead me through it and out the other side. His promise to me is an anointing for the occasion. "He has anointed my head with oil" over and over again. For this or that ministry I know I have needed the Spirit's touch, a lifting out of my dull "Mrs. Briscoe-ness" into an exciting awareness that my humanity has been touched by His divinity, and that He can and will transform this one-time *sheep in shepherd's clothing* into a *shepherd in sheep's clothing!* I know, then, that there will be the needed authority, the undershepherd's touch of class, the smoothness, brightness and fragrance of oil on my lips. It is at times like this that my cup has indeed run over. What joy!

This is not to say I have always been a success. I can think of times that I have spoken untouched and unblessed. There have been occasions when the oil has not touched my lips, and my cup has been empty. But I have tried to fail successfully—to make sure there have not been too many of those experiences to grieve about, and I have found that goodness and mercy (God's good sheepdogs) have always been at my heels, ready to round me up and bring me back in touch. If I will only feast after failure, I will not fail for very long.

The most exacting part of my relationship with the Shepherd comes in the obedience that is a daily choice to follow fully; then other sheep that are not of this fold will be brought to Him. An eastern shepherd often uses his pet sheep, the one that follows him the very closest, to reach the sheep that are caught in the highest rocks and crevices, beyond the help of dog or human hands. I want very badly to be that special lamb. That is why I am willing to fail again and again on the way to learning faithfulness and followship. My

Lord, who is my Shepherd, has promised me that He will match my weak willingness with His sweet success.

> In heav'nly love abiding,
>   No change my heart shall fear;
> And safe is such confiding,
>   For nothing changes here.
> The storm may roar without me,
>   My heart may low be laid,
> But God is round about me,
>   And can I be dismayed?
>
> Wherever He may guide me,
>   No want shall turn me back;
> My Shepherd is beside me,
>   And nothing can I lack.
> His wisdom ever waketh,
>   His sight is never dim;
> He knows the way He taketh,
>   And I will walk with Him.
>
> Green pastures are before me,
>   Which yet I have not seen;
> Bright skies will soon be o'er me,
>   Where the dark clouds have been.
> My hope I cannot measure;
>   My path to life is free;
> My Saviour has my treasure,
>   And He will walk with me.

ANNA L. WARING

WORKSHEET

Shaggy Sheep

Suggested time—5 minutes

1. Read the following verses:
   Isaiah 1:18 and Isaiah 53:6; put them in your own words.

Suggested time—6 minutes

2. How "good" are you at doing things "badly"? (Colossians 3:23).
   How can a *fear of failure* affect our Christian lives? Discuss.

Suggested time—10 minutes

3. Read Psalm 23 and underline it in the following way:
   Something about God—green
   Something about me —brown
   Promises   —yellow
   Commands   —blue
   Warnings   —red
   Choose a verse that speaks to you and underline it in pink.
   Share your findings with the group.

Suggested time—3 minutes

4. Why is it so important to make sure we do not fail to walk in
   "right" paths? (Psalms 23:3).

Suggested time—5 minutes

5. Discuss:
   a) How God can help us overcome the fear of failure.
   b) How we can help each other.
   c) How we can help ourselves.

Suggested time—5 minutes

6. Share a "broken-leg" experience. (*Keep it short!*)

Suggested time—10 minutes

7. Read John 10:1–16 and make a list of all the things the Good Shepherd will not fail to do for His sheep.
(Example: verse 3—The Shepherd talks to His sheep.)

Suggested time—5 minutes

8. Do you believe that
    a) failure is never final?
    b) Christ gives us freedom to fail?

Suggested time—5 minutes

9. Prayer Time
Pray about the things you have learned.

2
Foolish Followers

Dead flies cause the ointment of the apothecary to send forth a stinking savour: so doth a little folly him that is in reputation for wisdom and honour.

Ecclesiastes 10:1

This is a story about how a fly in the ointment can cause a big stink.

God is the Great Apothecary, the Confectioner of heavenly ointments. Such commodities are comprised of a butter tallow unguent, like oil. The ancient perfumers made use of the well-known power of oils and fats to absorb and give off odors. For example, olive oil formed the composition of the holy anointing oil used in the tabernacle, mentioned in Exodus 30:23–25. The oil base was then scented with liquid myrrh, fragrant cinnamon, cane, and sweet cassia.

This holy oil was to be prepared by the high priest Eleazar, or in later times by the sons of the priests (1 Chronicles 9:30). Anyone else attempting to make it was to be punished (Exodus 30:33). The Great Apothecary provided the raw ingredients for the base of all ointments, but the priests of God had the responsibility of mixing it with herbs to complete the confection. The end result was to be a sweet savor of worship that would please the heart of God. The perfumed incense made by the priests represented the loving self-sacrifice of God's people, as they brought themselves and their offerings to the altar.

Ecclesiastes tells us that a man's reputation is like the base ointment. It has the power to absorb and give off savors. This is common to men everywhere and not just to believers in Christ. God has given a reputation to every single human being living on the face of this earth. The ensuing savor or smell will depend very much upon the mixture of herbs that a man drops into the base oil of his character.

Did you know you can drop *Christ,* the finest, freshest, most fragrant herb of all into your character? And when Christ comes into your life, others will sense His presence by just being near you! Paul says in Corinthians that through Christians, "God spreads everywhere the fragrance of the knowledge of him" (2 Corinthians 2:14 NIV). He says that we are, to God, the aroma of Christ among those who are being saved and those who are perishing. He means that we cannot hide the fact that Christ has come. We can keep our mouths shut about it, but that won't stop the fragrance of God's Son invading the atmosphere around us. As Beatrice Cleland puts it:

> Not only by the words you say, not only in your
>   deeds confessed,
> But in the most unconscious way is Christ
>   expressed.
> Is it a beatific smile, a holy light upon your
>   brow?
> Oh, no! I felt His presence when you laughed
>   just *now.*
> For me, 'twas not the truth you taught, to you
>   so clear, to me so dim,
> But when you came to me, you brought a sense
>   of Him.
> And from your eyes He beckons me, and from your
>   lips His love is shed,
> Till I lose sight of you and see the Christ
>   instead.

"Indwelt"

It is that fragrant, mysterious, and yet unmistakable "sense of Him" that I am talking about. This is not to say we needn't talk about our faith, at all. We are told explicitly in the Scriptures, that if we have received Christ, we are to testify "with our mouths" to that fact (*see* Romans 10:9). But this aroma of Christ I speak about is a discernible fragrance that smells like nothing else! It delights the heart of God and enchants the senses of those who love Him, but at the same time, and in some strange way, it distresses and disturbs those who know Him not. It has the power to make such people remove themselves as far away from us as possible, for "To the one we are the smell of death; to the other, the fragrance of life . . . (2 Corinthians 2:16 NIV).

I have been in church and seen unbelieving people come out from a service, complaining that they didn't like the atmosphere. When pressed to explain their comments, they have been at a loss for words, but have eventually said something like, "Can't you sense it? I don't know what it is about this church and these people, but it makes me sick!" For them the aroma of Christ has been the very smell of death. It is death to the one who does not wish to be rescued from perishing. He worries that if he stays around he may catch the disease and die, which is a really strange anomaly. The smell of life—to the one who is perishing—is the smell of death. On the other hand, the smell of life—to one who is being saved—is the smell of life.

The week after Christ came into my heart, I noticed that my friends were acting in the strangest way. They really didn't want to be around me anymore. I would catch them glancing furtively over their books at me, or peering across the lounge with puzzled expressions on their faces. Was it something I had said? I worried. But then I had not yet dared to share my new experience with them, so I knew it couldn't be that. And yet it *was* that! It was not exactly my experience, but the aroma of the Christ of my experience that was causing the problem. My friends were not used to the savor of a cleansed, forgiven personality—especially when it was exuding from someone like me. But this is the birthright of every born-again believer and the base of his newfound faith in Jesus Christ.

Maybe the same sort of thing has happened to you. Perhaps you have just come to know Jesus Christ as your Saviour, and you cannot understand the reaction of those who are closest to you. Well, now *that* is the problem, you see! They are closest to you, and therefore not able to avoid smelling the fresh aroma of His life. You will find that those who want to love Christ for themselves will be drawn to you by that fragrance, but those who do not will be driven away. To three of my friends, the fragrance of Jesus was the smell of death, and they kept away from me; but another close friend was fascinated. She actually asked me if I was wearing perfume, because she had noticed something almost undefinable about me that she had never noticed before. I do not intend you to think that this fragrance of which I speak can actually be smelled—I am really talking of a spiritual awareness, not a natural one. That "something" my friend had noticed was of course a *Someone*—the Christ who is a sweet aroma to God and to those who are being saved. Shortly afterwards, she came to know the Great Apothecary's Son for herself.

This cleansed new ointment and the fragrance of the Christ who has cleansed it has been offered as a gift to the forgiven sinner. To be given another chance! Oh, joy! I can remember moving house and home after the war. We had lived in the beautiful English lake district during the hard years, but now the confrontation was past, and we were returning to Liverpool. My big sister cried copiously, as we traveled toward that great city in the industrial north, for she had loved her Wordsworth's land; the seas of golden daffodils, the languid lakes, the hilly hills—so many of the Mighty's masterpieces.

There were no such tears on my face, for even though I was only nine years of age, I can well remember wanting very badly to start all over again. *No one knows me in Liverpool,* I thought excitedly. I had another chance to make friends and keep them, play games and win them, and work for grades and get them. Not one soul knew about my past (all nine years of it), so now it was all up to me. But after another ten years of losing friends, games, and grades, I was back to square one. Experiencing the same old hope for a whole new change, I stood next on the platform of a train station waving good-bye to my parents, while saying hello to Cambridge! Surely no one would know about me there, I thought. Now I could have one more try. But it wasn't very long until I had had my try and my hopes had faded again, and this time there was nowhere else to go. Can you possibly imagine therefore what a verse like 2 Corinthians 5:17 meant to me?

Therefore, if anyone is in Christ, he is a new creation; the old has gone, the new has come!

NIV

I had wanted so badly to become wise—after all, that's why I had come to Cambridge—but I discovered I was held in reputation as a fool, and even though I had hotly sought for honor, I had failed to be even elected for the place of twelfth officer of my class! I came to the frightening realization that it was not going to be a new city school or friend that was going to make the difference, because wherever I moved I took *me!* Wherever I lived, there had always been a fly in the ointment, and I couldn't seem to stop making a big stink as soon as I settled in. I reminded me of the family that fled the dreaded plague of London. Settling in a city far away from the capital, they fell victim to the disease anyway, not realizing that they had carried some infected flies with them in their clothing. And not only did the family catch the plague, they brought death to everyone else around them. This seemed to be my case, and I began to despair of ever knowing anything else.

However, now I had come to know Christ; the "new had come." For those who invite Fresh Faithfulness into their hearts to stay, a whole new way of life begins. For me, receiving Christ into the character base of my life meant that I could settle down in the place of my failure and begin to succeed. Now I did not need to move on to a different city, acquire a fresh group of friends and attend a new school every four or five years. I could stay right where I was, because God had given me a brand-new start.

As if that wasn't enough, God invested me with the fantastic privilege of priesthood. Remember it was the priests of God who were to mix the holy ointment for the worship hour. Now it was up to me to gather the heavenly herbs of wisdom and honor, and mixing them in the base of my new reputation, please the heart of God.

Our text has to do with him who is in reputation for wisdom and honor (Ecclesiastes 10:1). Once God has cleansed our character and made us just as if we'd never sinned, it is just as if the fly of Christlessness has never been there at all. He expects us to begin to develop a new, lasting reputation. A spiritual reputation does not mean we try to be spiritually clever, but rather that we strive to be spiritually wise. There is a great difference. We must search for this wisdom as the perfumer sought for the herbs, and it begins with the fear of the Lord (Proverbs 1:7). The fear of the Lord does not mean a feeling of intimidation where God is concerned, but rather carries the sense of a reverent awe, coupled with a hatred of evil. It means growing to love everything that He loves, and beginning to hate anything that He hates.

To be spiritually wise is to be sensitive to dead flies and never allow them to fly into the ointment. It means also the accumulation of spiritual facts about spiritual realities and a knowledge of how to put the new information to work in our everyday lives. It is in the day-to-day business of our day-to-day doings that we are to earn our new reputations. We need spiritual wisdom to behave as spiritual people—wives, husbands, mothers, fathers, daughters, sons, mothers-in-law, fathers-in-law, grandmothers and grandfathers— and the Bible tells us that ". . . Christ who is wisdom has been made over to us for that purpose (*see* Colossians 2:2, 3). Spiritual wisdom comes with an ever-deepening relationship with Him, and as we work at that we shall find, perhaps to our surprise, that we begin to have a "good" reputation. We shall come to be known as caring counselors, reliable friends, kind doers of good deeds, people of integrity, trustworthy folks, and, in fact, good solid citizens!

After I was born again, I began to notice that people began to come to me for advice. Before this, I had tried to give my advice away but with little success. Now I found friends at college beating a path to my door to ask questions—not that I knew the answers, but somehow the *fragrance* had spread around, and people got to sense I loved what He loved and hated what He hated, and apparently they wanted to *savor* that! People told me that they noticed I had changed—for the better—they added hastily! I was easier to live with and more fun to have around, gentler and sweeter with a lot more sense, they said.

They must have told other people as well as telling me, and honor followed. (Honor is the value that others attribute to a person who is earning a new and wise reputation.) Honor says that a person is worthy of respect, that he has earned the right to be listened to, and is well regarded by his peers. "Them that honour me I will honour," said the Lord in 1 Samuel 2:30. It's quite true He does. As we work hard as God's priests, mixing the herbs of wisdom and honor into our new reputation, and as we learn to obey Scripture, honoring God, as self-sacrificing servants of the Lord; as we yield honor to king and country, widows, and to all to whom honor is due, we will find the people we treat in this way will return the compliment and begin to respect and appreciate us. It is in this way that Christian character is formed and godly reputations are established, and it is in this way that men are made aware of Him.

If we are being honored by men for our spiritual wisdom, you may be sure the glory will go to the Great Apothecary Himself, for people well know such wisdom is certainly not our own. As they see us demonstrating a new respect for authority, a new love for our wives or husbands, a new submission to our parents, and new care for the poor, they will know we have become new people, indeed. Then those who know us best will add their word of witness to ours, acknowledging the fact that we couldn't have cared less before we cared for Christ!

Shortly after I became the Lord's, I discovered a strange new sensation inside. Before this time, I had always reluctantly obeyed people in authority (while grumbling about it behind their backs), but now I found I really wanted to please. I didn't want to say anything behind those people I wouldn't say in front of them! That was quite a change for me, I can tell you. I discovered the strange, new sensation I was experiencing was called *love*, and as I added love to honor, mixing these two heavenly herbs into the ointment, I realized I had value in other people's eyes. People knew I really respected them now, and they began to respect me back!

Then I found myself beginning to care for the poor. Oh, not the *poor* poor, like the skinny, starved babies gawking at us from the hunger posters, but the street poor of Liverpool, my own hometown. I had lived in Liverpool all my teenage life but I had never cared for the poor. I didn't respect, appreciate, or honor them! But now it was different. After teaching school all day, I found myself out on the streets haunting the bombed sites, coffee bars, and teenage hangouts—wanting desperately to get near enough to touch those kids and tell them they were important to God and to me. Because they saw they were important to me, they began to hope they were important to God, and eventually they began to believe that if what they *did* mattered to me, it mattered to Him also. It wasn't long before God began to spread the sweet aroma of Christ around the back streets of Liverpool, through some street-wise kids who were now becoming spiritually wise as well!

Can you see, then, that a Christian who has begun well (by learning to know his Saviour and Lord, and by establishing a growing reputation for spiritual wisdom), and who begins to be honored by his peers, must most carefully watch for dead flies! It seems absolutely unthinkable to me that such people could allow a fly to get into the ointment! But, alas, we know from our own bitter experience and the spoiled testimony of others how easily the sweet, sweet savor can turn to a sour, sad smell. For: "Dead flies cause the ointment of the apothecary to send forth a stinking savour: so doth a little folly him that is in reputation for wisdom and honour" (Ecclesiastes 10:1). In fact, the smell seems one hundred times worse, if someone has really been doing well as a Christian, and *then* succumbs to the flies. If this happens, we "fail to be fragrant," and cannot hide the whole, sad state of affairs from the world.

I remember the shock it was to me to have one of the young people I had been working with tell me how carefully she was watching me. Until she grew up in God, I sensed the huge responsibility I carried not to stumble that little one in any way by my behavior. This is not to say we must be perfect. God does not expect that of us until we awake in heaven "with His likeness." We are not required to be models of perfection, but we are expected to be models of growth, and if we have any position of leadership whatever within the Christian community, we bear the responsibility to be constantly looking out for dead flies.

So what are some of these *dead flies* that can drop into the Apothecary's ointment? The text is explicit: "a little folly" is like dead flies. Now just a "little" fly is all that is needed. The base changes not. The oil does not cease to have the capacity to absorb, retain, and give off other savors, simply because the Christ has been added to it. And so a tiny fly—just a little black speck—will be all that is needed to do the trick. Just a *little folly*. That's all! What is folly? Folly is the good old-fashioned word for foolishness. A little foolishness is like a dead fly.

Most Christians I know would not allow the big fly of adultery, rape, theft, or murder to foul them up. But many Christians I know (including myself) have to deal not so much with the blue-tail fly, but with the little bugs—the itty-bitty things that don't look as though they would matter at all. There is the fly of *flirting* for example. Flirting is a habit of looking at a member of the opposite sex and inviting investigation. It is using your sexuality to try and control another person, whom you have no right to control. It's just a little fly, but, oh, what a big stink the end of that adventure can bring! Ask David and Bathsheba about that. Bathsheba's husband was out of town, and she was lonely. She couldn't help but be aware that King David had stayed at home, and did so at a time "when kings went forth to war"! David stayed in bed all day long, but got up in time to take a walk on the flat eastern rooftop and spot beautiful Bathsheba taking a bath. The dead fly of laziness was already in David's ointment, but now it was joined by a swarm of flies including lies, adultery, and murder. There is no need to tell you about the stink that caused in Israel, in David's and Bathsheba's personal lives, and in the eyes of those who held David in reputation for wisdom and honor!

We should be more than mildly concerned at this present time about the casual way Christians guard their marriage relationships. The divorce statistics have come to church, and we are seeing Sunday-school teachers, choir members, youth leaders, and even preachers divorcing their wives. Women are going back to work, by the thousands, and whether they go naively unprepared for the big, cold, sex-orientated world or not, I don't know. What I do know is that many of the new work force are Christian women, and they go with sweet fragrant reputations that are fouled up in no time at all because they allow a little fly of foolishness to land in the ointment.

It only takes a *little* fly, remember. A little look, a little ride home, a little touch, a little squeeze of the hand, a little flirtation, a little lunch, a little phone call, a little letter. Those of us who have the incredible privilege of a Christian marriage are not exempt from temptation. An old Chinese proverb says, "You can't stop the birds flying over your head, but you can stop them from nesting in your hair." Or in the figure we are using to illustrate our point: "You can't stop the flies from buzzing around your head, but you can stop them from falling in the ointment." We can watch the way we dress, the way we conduct ourselves, the way we look at people, the way we hold a conversation, and we can avoid being put in compromising situations, or taking a job where sexual favors are insinuated. We can stop enjoying a little flattery and learn to be stern with ourselves concerning the *little* book we read or the *little* film we watch that feeds our desires and leaves us hungry for more—especially when our husbands are out of town, or we are out of town without them! There is a veritable plague of flies in the world today, and they are all bred by the lord of the flies himself, who is telling them where to land.

A watching world, antagonistic to God and His principles, is always on the lookout for trouble in the Christian camp, and when it sees the dead fly of sexual sin amongst Christian leadership, it says with disgust, "It stinks." This sort of sin brings the Great Apothecary to shame.

Then there is the fly of cheating. It's just a little fly. Just a little glance on a little test, in a little school in a little town, on a little day. But I tell you it's a *big* day for the devil when the world catches a Christian kid cheating. "It stinks," it says triumphantly. But think how hard it is for our Christian youngsters, when everyone else is getting a better mark than they are, because they are cheating and getting away with it. I am told by many students from different campus situations that cheating is a way of life. Everybody cheats. But that's not true. Christians don't. Cheating doesn't build a reputation for wisdom or honor. You may not be thanked for being honest; in fact you may well be persecuted for it, because your very honesty can get others into trouble, but you have no option. It's a wise thing in the end to be a man or a woman of integrity and tell the truth, play it straight, and mix the herb of honesty into the oil of your character.

When my husband started work in a bank at the age of seventeen, his boss took a liking to him, and was soon leaving him with lots of responsibility. The senior official began to leave the office more and more during working hours, and one day he told Stuart to tell anyone that called for him that he was busy.

"Will you be busy, sir?" inquired his young trainee. "No," snapped his boss, "I will be out, but that's not your business. You tell anyone that calls that I'm busy!"

It was not an easy thing for that seventeen-year-old boy to do, but he said, "I'm sorry, sir, I won't tell a lie for you—and I'll tell you why. If I told a lie *for* you how would you know I would not tell a lie *to* you? This way you will be able to bank on me always telling you the truth!"

He could have lost his job (and perhaps today he would have), but the manager respected him for that stand and held him in honor for it. It turned out to be the wisest thing for him to do because he was subsequently trusted with great career opportunities. Of course, we don't do the wise and honest thing because we may get promoted, but because "all things have become new," and our responsibility is to keep them that way.

Then there's the repulsive odor, when a believing teammate succumbs to peer pressure and gets drunk after the football game. It all starts with just a *little* folly—just a little drink, in a little bar, in a little town. But a little folly is too much folly, because a little folly is like "dead flies causing the ointment of the apothecary to send forth a stinking savor!" The problem is that a little fly causes as much trouble as a big fly, and we find out that it's not really the size that matters, because the ointment is spoiled, one way or the other—and *that's* what matters! Instead of bringing a fresh fragrance of a life of worship to a stale world, we find ourselves causing one big stink. To be really blunt—we fail to be fragrant, and *smell* instead!

Our text gives me to understand that the one who mixes the ointment is responsible for the result. The confection that I make from
the base of my new reputation is my responsibility. The sons of the
priest were told that they, and they alone, must tend the "incense."
If they failed, or expected someone else to do it for them, then they
were to be cut off from their people. Knowing that a fresh fragrance
is required to please and honor the Great Apothecary, people fail to
tend the ointment. Having failed, they then find they are really in
trouble, and many are cut off from the church because of this. Some
have started their Christian lives well: witnessing to their friends,
reading the Bible every day, joining a church, and are well on the
way to building a sure and honorable reputation. People have even
begun to respect them for their new life-style, except, perhaps, for a
few acquaintances who smelled the smell of death and have disappeared.

Now, however, the young Christian fails to fend off the flies. One
after another the dead things drop into the ointment, and even the
Christian friends begin to fall away. Once all the friends, new and
old, have disappeared, it's a whole bad scene. But take courage. I
believe that there is help for you. The Great Apothecary won't disappear. This is, in fact, just why I have written this book. I wanted
to help and to remind you of that. I wrote it for people who fail.
People like you and people like me and people like people! There is
not one human being on the face of God's earth who hasn't had a
fly in the ointment at one time or another! No, not *one!* Just in case
you think you are the exception, God confirms this fact of universal
failure from the Scriptures: ". . . there is none that doeth good, no,
not one" (Romans 3:12).

The idea is to come and kneel at the feet of Jesus. Ask Him to
help you to keep the fragrance fresh—to shut out the flies, so you
can please the heart of God. Mary of Bethany knew all about ointment. She had an alabaster box full of it. It was very costly, very
fragrant, and very important. The lid had been kept tightly shut; in
fact the box had to be broken to release the gift. She knew very well
that flies must not be allowed to get into it; but she also knew it
would be far safer spilled out in a loving act of sacrifice at Jesus'

feet, rather than her trying to safeguard it all by herself. We cannot fend off the flies without the assistance of our Lord. He is our Saviour. He did not die only for our iniquity before we knew His saving power, but for the sins we have committed since we have known Him. We need to give our reputations as Christians to Him, that He may keep them safe and sound. We must be aware that to keep our alabaster box of ointment locked up in an inner room of our lives, believing we can guard it ourselves is not the best way of going about things; neither is it the safest. Thieves can break through and steal such hidden treasures. The best place for our ointment is at the feet of Jesus. Kneeling there, we must give it to Him.

Once the priests in Old Testament times had mixed the ointment, it was offered to the Lord in worship. We can come to Him in prayer and remind ourselves that, but for the grace of God, we would still be lost with Christless reputations—a savor of death. We can kneel, remembering the cross and the One who went there to make it possible to cleanse our hearts and lives and give us a new start. We can pour out that new start—that cleansed reputation at His feet, acknowledging we will need Him to help us do our part. If I am speaking to new believers who have just started to build a new reputation of wisdom and honor, take heed concerning dead flies; guard your new life, and don't try to do it without living in an attitude of dependence on Jesus Christ. This way and this way only can the fragrance of the ointment fill the house (John 12:3). In giving the ointment to Jesus, Mary's reputation was assured. Jesus said that what she had done would be talked about forever, and her reputation would spread the wide world over (Matthew 26:13). He said she would be honored by all men everywhere.

Let us strive to be like Mary. And for those who read this chapter who are deeply troubled by all of this; those of you who have been Christians for years and think no one else knows about the fly in your ointment—be advised! You may *think* nobody knows, but everybody really does. They are aware something is wrong, because there is a certain "savor of death" emanating from your life. You cannot stop it, for remember that oil has that quality—it retains and gives off odors. In the following chapters, I will try to give you hope to start again. No matter how big a stink you have caused, and no matter what huge fly is in your ointment, I believe the Great Apothecary can put it right. But first the whole "box" needs to be given to Him. The entire affair, whether it be an illicit relationship, some stolen goods, a vicious letter—all must be poured out at His feet. This is where a new fresh fragrance starts.

This doesn't mean the world will forgive us for making the bad smell in the first place. The world seldom, if ever, does. Bad odors are remembered for an awfully long time. It might even take the church as long as it takes the world to forgive us. But a new, sweet fragrant scent helps people to start to forget the bad savor.

Failure is never final where the Christian is concerned. The fly in the ointment can be removed by the grace and with the help of the Great Apothecary.

Will you not do your priestly work, collect the heavenly herbs, mix them with repentance, and faith, and adoration—and worship?

>"Within the Veil": be this,
>   belov'd, thy portion,
>Within the secret of thy Lord to
>   dwell;
>Beholding Him, until thy face His
>   glory,
>   Thy life His love, thy lips His praise
>   shall tell.
>
>"Within the Veil," for only as thou
>   gazest
>Upon the matchless beauty of His
>   face,
>Canst thou become a living revelation
>   Of His great heart of love, His
>   untold grace.
>
>"Within the Veil," His fragrance
>   poured upon thee,
>Without the Veil, that fragrance
>   shed abroad;

"Within the Veil," His hand shall
tune the music
Which sounds on earth the praises
of thy Lord.

"Within the Veil," thy spirit deeply
anchored,
Thou walkest calm above a world of
strife;
"Within the Veil" thy soul with
Him united,
Shall live on earth His resurrection
life.

FREDA H. ALLEN

WORKSHEET

Foolish Followers

Suggested time—6 minutes

1. Review what these pictures can represent:
   The Great Apothecary
   The base perfume
   The priests
   The savors
   The herbs
   Dead flies

Suggested time—6 minutes

2. Read 2 Corinthians 2:14–16. Discuss:
   a) Have you ever sensed the Christ's presence in someone else's life? Share.
   b) How do we build a healthy reputation for wisdom and honor? (*Read Colossians 2:2, 3.*)

Suggested time—10 minutes

3. Discuss some of the flies in the ointment that can cause a big stink.
   If divided by twos, share about a dead fly you are trying to fend off at this present time; ask your partner to pray about it for you. (*Share only if appropriate.*)

Suggested time—15 minutes

4. Read Luke 7:36–39.
   a) What does this story say about the Christ?
   b) About Mary?
   c) About you?

Suggested time—5 minutes

5. Prayer Time
   Read Ecclesiastes 10:1 again. Think about it in silence.
   Spend a few minutes alone with the Great Apothecary.

3

Crumbling Clay

*But now, O Lord, thou art our father; we are the clay, and
thou our potter; and we all are the work of thy hand.*

Isaiah 64:8

This is about pot people, mud men, dust dollies—and how to avoid becoming a limp lump!

His hands formed the dry land, the light and the darkness. In the beginning, every beast of the field was fashioned by His fingers, even the grasshopper (Psalms 95:5; Isaiah 45:7; Genesis 2:19; Amos 7:1). I speak of the Potter, who formed and made me also (Psalms 119:73). When the little dust man that the Lord had formed from the ground rebelled against Him, God determined he should return from whence he came! " . . . dust thou art, and unto dust thou shall return," He said to Adam in Genesis 3:19.

Nobody questions the fact that our bodies return to dust after death, and yet some people have a real problem believing that their living bodies are comprised of mere clay. They think that even the Bible is highly suspect for saying so. A physicist told me, however, that there is no conflict with science on this point, and that man's body is, indeed, made up of elements found in his environment—a mere ten dollars worth to be exact, taking inflation into account! Our bodies are comprised (in part) of calcium, phosphorus, potassium, sulfur, sodium—one or two other ingredients (maybe a dash of salt and pepper?) and the rest—water.

This is not to say the body is to be taken lightly. We are surely fearfully and wonderfully made. You can always judge a potter by his pottery, and what divinity has done with dust defies description. It will need only a brief illustration to show that we are indeed created by a fantastic Potter. The messages in our brains are carried by electrical impulses and relayed to minute computer centers, linked by wirelike connections called *dendrites*. A scientist told me that if these dendrites were stretched end to end, they would reach to the moon and back. And all that is complete in a baby's nervous system, while still in its mother's womb. Yes, you can always judge a potter by his pottery!

We need to treat this incredible pot with the care and dignity that God affords it. If He took all that trouble making it, we need to spend a little time tending it—and yet we need to keep our perspective too—for after all is said and done, the body is only a *pot*. Though important, it must never be allowed to become *all*-important. In Old Testament times, a pot's worth was determined by its carrying capacity, and the body, though marvelously and wonderfully made, was really fashioned to carry something of much greater worth than itself. It was created to contain one of the greatest of all of God's treasures—the human spirit. This spiritual part of us was also fashioned by the Potter. It is Zechariah who tells us that:

> ... the Lord, which stretcheth forth the heavens, and layeth the foundation of the earth, and formeth the spirit of man within him.

> Zechariah 12:1

So we are not *only* little pot people, dust dollies, mud men running around a little clay earth. The Divine Potter has planned a holy function for the pot. He has deemed it proper to make our earthen vessels the Spirit's home. It is the spirit of man that is capable of receiving and housing the Spirit of God. Paul spoke of his body as the temple of the Holy Spirit, and everyone knows that a temple is a sacred place. When men and women and boys and girls understand that their bodies have been created by the Lord to nourish and cherish the human spirit, that in itself has the capacity to contain God, then they begin to view and treat people with a new respect. For example, this viewpoint makes a huge difference to the way a boy behaves toward a girl. If a man believes that a woman is not merely a body, but that a woman *has* a body, created by God for a holy purpose, then he will handle her as a piece of divine creation, realizing he will be answerable to God for his treatment of her. When a man does not believe that a woman is anything more than a womb, or a well-equipped incubator, he will treat her as a thing and not as a person. The very fact that we have been made by God for God should lend us dignity, but the knowledge that we are *like* God should make us even more careful in our attitude toward ourselves and each other.

God is a Spirit, and in this sense we are like Him. It is because man is a spiritual being, that pot appetites, comforts, or thrills can never make him happy for very long. The deeper spiritual realm must be explained, experienced, and explored if there is to be real fulfillment. But God is not only a spiritual being, He is eternal too, and He fashioned us after His image in this way also. This is why our spirits are restless and searching, until they come to grips with eternal realities. We are conscious from our earliest days of a Being outside ourselves "somewhere." We "know" that there is something after death—and that when we are dead, we are not done with; we know these things because we are *eternal* beings. God is also a rational being; He is mind, and He is omniscient. He knows and understands Himself completely and all others perfectly. If I have indeed been engraved with His likeness, then I have the special capacity to thoroughly understand myself and others more perfectly. The Christian has also received the mind of Christ (1 Corinthians 2:16), and therefore has the ability to know God as Christ knows Him! Once this happens to a human being, he has no trouble answering the age-old questions: *Who am I; why am I; where am I;* or *who is God; where is God,* and *why is God?*

But God is not just *mind*; He has feelings, too. We know He is an emotional being, for we have seen God, in Christ—laughing, weeping, and rejoicing, as He lived amongst us. Since we have been made in His image, we too possess the ability to express ourselves emotionally. We can care, laugh, weep, and rejoice. Then God has revealed Himself to us as a volitional being. This means He can reason and make moral judgments. In other words, He is a responsible moral personality, knowing perfectly well what is right and what is wrong. So are we! We can try smothering our consciences (if we will), but since He made us like Himself, we find we perfectly well know what is good and what is evil, what is right and what is wrong. We somehow are aware that there are such things as *absolutes*. We are cognizant of the fact that there are certain standards that He has set for us, and that He fully expects us to adhere to them. And human beings *know* all these things without being brainwashed by a Christian culture.

I can testify to that. For eighteen years I never attended church, read the Bible, or talked with committed believers, but there was not one moment of that time that I was not deeply aware of the divine plumb line of truth and error, right and wrong, good and evil. I *knew!* And what's more: I *knew* He knew I knew! Even though we are fallen immoral beings, we are perfectly capable of making moral judgments, because we have been created as beings corresponding to the Original. In other words, we have the Potter's personality stamped on our spiritual features.

Let me illustrate this for you. We have three children, of whom David is the eldest. He is tidy, disciplined, and wastes absolutely nothing. Judy, our second child, is intense and meticulous; a bright overachiever. Pete is our comedian—good company, slightly zany, and an excellent communicator! All three of them attended the same pottery class at school. The pots they made are sitting on my shelf, watching me, as I write this very story about them. A friend who knows the family well has just left the room, but not before I asked her if she could tell me which child made which pot. Without any hesitation she correctly identified their work.

"This one belongs to Dave," she said, pointing to a neat little jug with a tidy appearance. "This is Judy's," she said, picking up a marvelously intricate vase with no end of precise and mathematically calculated patterning on it; and, "This—this has to be Pete's," she laughed, fingering a funny crooked jug with a huge nose at least three inches long sticking out of one side of it. She was right, of course, because the personalities of the three small potters had been indelibly impressed upon the clay. Their express image was there for all to see.

The Lord God formed us and made us like Himself, and we carry with us in our very personalities His very likeness. The word *image* is the same word that is used for a particular engraving tool that the potter uses to write his name upon his special workmanship. We have the imprint of His initials in our hearts.

Then how is it, we may well ask, that the clay is marred? How can it be that the Potter's personality seems so obscured? When I look around me in this wild and woolly world, and when I look within me at my twisted, taut reactions to the good, I know that something must have gone drastically wrong with the Potter's plans. That is so. Believe it or not, there came a day when the little clay man shook his little clay fist in the Great and Eternal Potter's face and sinned.

> The thing formed said of Him,
>   Who formed it, "You know nothing."
> The work said of Him who made it,
>   "You made me not."

See Isaiah 29:16

Dust that could not possibly be independent decided so to be. Dust that is dependent on a supernatural force to keep it sticking together decided it could stop itself from falling apart, and this— even though the Bible tells us "*by Him*" all things consist or stick together. How God must have laughed, as He heard dust talking, saying, We don't need the Potter:

> Our own self-sufficiency will keep
>   us from falling apart—
>   Our own dust minds and
>   dust abilities—
>
> It is well that God did not say, Puff! and
>   watch dust fly away!

But He knew that little dust people would be dependent on climate, dust food and shelter, and on dust health.

He understood that germs love dust and that it would be a lifelong battle to keep them at bay.

God being perfect health, must have been very amused at the little dust people, who chose to rely on bottles of dust pills advertised on

dust television and seldom asked the source of all health to shine His
rays into their dust bodies and heal their diseases.

What a ridiculous situation when dependent dust became independent, thinking it could figure out the universe, understand all mysteries, solve all riddles, and ingeniously learn to manipulate atoms so that it could blow up all the other little dust people in the world!

JILL BRISCOE
Adapted from *There's a Snake in My Garden*

Independence, which is the very essence of sin, marred the clay. It will ever be a mystery that the clay was spared at all, and that the Potter was gracious enough to offer to make it all over again. But mystery or not, we are told that He decided to put His hands on any lump of crumbling clay that would ask Him to, and work with it, until a whole new entity appeared.

I know of no other craft where the craftsman gets so thoroughly and personally involved with his material than the craft of pottery. In my mind's eye, I envisage the potter up to his elbows in the sticky stuff, as he remakes, reshapes, and remodels it. Nearly two thousand years ago, the Mighty Potter became terribly and personally involved with His marred material, and we need to remind ourselves of the cost of that redemptive remodeling. The hands of the Potter were horribly mutilated in the process—nail pierced to be exact—and you can't get much more involved with your material than that! But the Potter had thought of a grand and glorious plan you see, even before the clay had ever become marred. He had devised a way the vessels could escape His wrath and be fitted for glory, rather than destruction. He made a way to remake them all over again. He decided that His treasure, the Lord Jesus, could be invited into the earthen vessels to accomplish the needed transformation; this way the final firing of death would mean that they would not be vitrified forever in their rebellious shape.

The word *vitrified* is used to describe what happens to a pot after it has been finally fired. It means "set forever" and gives us a graphic and ghastly picture of a personality set in concrete by hell's heat. The Bible clearly tells us that there will be no changing after that experience, for the fire of His wrath immobilizes the personality, allowing no possibility of change thereafter (Hebrews 9:27). The person in that case can never become "like Him" after death, because they will have been set already in an everlasting shape of self-ishness. It is only while we are still alive and by the Lord Jesus' transforming power that any of us can be fitted for glory. Have we been made over? Have we received Jesus into our earthen pots? If so, we have already been fitted for glory! What is more, He has had us on His eternal mind and has written our names into His eternal book.

A potter has a manual. He may start many new pieces, but each work is kept in mind and carefully cataloged. This is because he has specific plans for each piece. Before he ever begins working a piece of clay, the pot is already finished in his mind and has been entered carefully in his records. He has recorded the chemical formula, the glaze used, the temperature at which it will be fired, and for how long. We know the Heavenly Potter has a manual because the psalmist tells us so in Psalms 139:16:

> Thine eyes did see my substance, yet being unperfect; and in thy book all my members were written, which in continuance were fashioned, when as yet there was none of them.

Many people have a terrible problem with self-worth. They don't believe they are valuable. This is one of the biggest reasons people fail to be what they are *intended* to be. They do not have a good self-image, are down on themselves, unsure of how to behave in company, and embarrassed with their own appearance or performance. What a transformation can take place in a heart and life when a person comes to know the Potter and reads Psalm 139. What encouragement! To know we have been *heavily* on the mind of God surely gives us a sense of worth—especially when we realize that God has never had a thought He hasn't already had. To suppose He *suddenly* thought us up would be to suggest that there was a moment in time He hadn't thought of us at all, and since God has been revealed as a God who knows everything from the ages to the ages, He is acutely aware of every thought He has ever or will ever have. Therefore, there has never been a moment in all eternity that we have been off His mind. Now that really should make us feel special!

How often we hear the little phrase "It's the thought that matters." We mean that it is the fact that someone took the time to think about us for a few minutes that touches us. What warm self-confidence should be generated, when we realize we have been written up in the Potter's manual, and that the formula of our unique makeup has been there forever, even to the details of the glazing and the temperature of the firing. If it is *the thought that matters,* we can know that *we* matter!

I have just had another birthday, and this one proved to be a hard one for me. Arriving at the ripe old age of forty-six, I caught myself thinking, "When I grow up I want to be . . .!" I realized I needed to come to terms with the fact that I had already, indeed, grown up. I also had to accept the hard fact that I wouldn't be able to be many of those things I have always somehow believed I would have time to be. Having become irritated with myself for being slow to accomplish things, forgetful of people's names, and breathless after running up and down even shallow stairs; and having seen myself reflected in one of those awful three-way mirrors in a swimsuit store, I had to return to God and read Psalm 139 all over again. I was reminded by the Potter that I am neither too young nor too old—I am, in fact, just the right age for all the things the Potter has had in mind for me, for:

> You saw me before I was born and scheduled every day of my life before I began to breathe. Every day was recorded in Your Book!
>
> Psalms 139:16 TLB

Resting on this statement of Scripture, I could accept my birthday and know that I am right on schedule. This means I won't fail to accept myself as I am. I can even stop panicking once a year when that certain time comes around, and I can cease to dread my own old age. I can know I will even be dead on time.

My self-esteem received another boost, when I realized that the Heavenly Potter does not have an assembly line. Each piece has been handmade; each pot is totally unique. Each is beautiful in its very own way, especially when standing on the right shelf, fulfilling the function the designer had in mind for it. For example, a pitcher should pour well, without dripping, have a handle that is easily grasped and strong enough to carry the weight it will hold. It has been made for a specific job.

God has shaped us within and without for the function of our future, having a specific place and use for us. He said of the apostle Paul ". . . he is a chosen vessel unto me, to bear my name before the Gentiles . . ." (Acts 9:15). This man was chosen for the function of his future and painted with the colors of his culture. Decorated with his Jewish heritage, and patterned by his marvelous education, he was glazed with a brilliant intellect, and fired in the furnace of necessary affliction. Everything that had gone to make up the man called "Saul of Tarsus" had already been recorded in the Potter's manual well before he was ever committed. He had been fashioned to sit on many a Gentile shelf and bear Christ's name before the heathen world of his day. There will be a shelf for you to sit on, too, and there will be a shelf for me. Maybe it will be in the home, raising our children, or in the office, building bridges of friendship with confused friends, or in the hospital, old people's home, or even in prison. There will be a shelf on which to settle and a reason for our being there. If we are not to fail to fulfill the Potter's purpose, we will need to remember we have been painted with the colors of our culture and shaped for the function of our future. We can then discover we have been uniquely handmade for the occasion.

I think of my own background. I couldn't possibly have known the open doors of ministry the colors of my Britishness would give me in the USA. I remember with thankfulness the unique training I received at college, and particularly my courses in speech and drama. Years after this patterning, I find myself suitably fitted for my present calling. American people apparently love to have me sitting on their shelves! Realizing they have accepted me as I am, I have been able to accept myself. This way I stopped feeling out of place and came instead to know I was needed and appreciated. Knowing His purposes helps us to submit to His processes. Life on the wheel, after all, can sometimes give us the impression that we are going round and round in circles getting nowhere. But this need not be true. If I know the Potter has a purpose in making us as we are, and putting us down where we are, then we must believe there is a process going on, as He makes us what He would ultimately have us to be. It is not an easy thing to submit to the remodeling process. We wonder apprehensively what He will need to do to us and with us to finish us off.

Let us think about the Potter's wheel of life. First of all, the clay must be pliable in His hands. As He works with the material, the Potter continually reaches out to a pan of water with a small sponge and bathes the moving piece of clay, so that the revolving shape slips smoothly between His hands. If the piece should become dry in the shaping, it will tear, or be pulled out of balance, because of the ensuing friction.

Wet clay! The first step in the finishing process. I cannot escape from the marvelous picture of grief that this brings to mind. Bathed in tears, the clay becomes pliable in the Potter's hands. I wonder if we can be shaped at all without some wet days along the way. I remember being shocked at a funeral by a remark from a so-called bright, shiny, brittle Christian: "Christians don't cry!" she tartly told the little widow, who had just lost her partner of forty-five years. "Then how come Jesus wept?" mumbled the little widow to me. I nodded and pointed out to the "dry" lady that Jesus was undoubtedly a good Christian, and He knew what it was to be bathed in tears. Disturbed at this not uncommon reaction from our friend, I went home and found a verse in the Bible that helped. It talked of ancient mourning habits of the bereaved, who would ceremoniously weep over a wineskin (which served as a bottle in those days), and then carry their grief to the tomb of their loved one, leaving it there.

". . . put thou my tears into thy bottle: are they not in thy book?" I
read (Psalms 56:8). Sitting down with wet clay in mind, I wrote:

TEARS

Tears talking
  pattering petition on the door of heaven,
    Let me in. . . .
wet misery,
  fountains of fury,
    rivers of recrimination
  tears tearing down the river bed of doubt—
    stopping at the throne. . . .

Bottled bereavement
  arranged by angels,
    given to the King!

God tilts the bottle carefully, over His book of remembrance
  letting the drops fall onto a clean page.

Transported in a tear drop
  translated into eloquence

My washing woe writes its words of wounded worry down.

Splashing sadness signs its name
  then dry depression comes to stay,
    for—all the tears have gone.

The Father reads my tears
  then passes the book to the Son,
    —Who shares it with the Spirit—

The angels gather round.
  Some small celestial cherubs
    are lifted to the Father's knees
    THE STORY IS TOLD

They listen—
  they all listen—
    I AM HEARD!

"I have heard her prayers, I have seen her tears,"
  —says the Father

"I am touched with the feelings of her infirmities,"
   —says the Son.

"I will pray for her with groanings which cannot be uttered,"
   —says the Spirit!

And God shall wipe all tears from her eyes
   sing the angels
And there shall be no more death
   neither sorrow nor crying,
Neither shall there be any more pain,
   for the former things *shall* pass away!

Yes, it is all right to cry, and it helps us to know when we do—that it is all part of the finishing process of "life on the wheel."

The Potter has a real job in hand because He not only has to keep us *pliable,* He also has to make sure He keeps us *centered.* This takes considerable strength, skill, and experience on His part. He knows, though, that if He cannot keep the whirling clay under tight control, it will go flying off the wheel, or develop into a small uneven piece of pottery. He wants very badly to finish up with a well-centered, balanced vessel. We fail to come to terms with His purpose for our lives, if we do not cooperate. We can refuse to allow Him to center us on the wheel and balance us up. So many Christians are unbalanced.

When I first became a believer, I went to so many extremes and frightened many of my friends away from Christianity with my slightly bizarre behavior. I decided that to become purely spiritual would mean becoming purely pure, and this left me no time or inclination to be normal or natural. Ignoring the verse in the Gospel of Luke that informed me that "Jesus increased in wisdom and stature, and in favour with God and man" (Luke 2:52), I concentrated solely on one aspect of development, that of increasing in favor with God, not realizing that this truly involved growing in all the other dimensions of my life as well. I stopped reading and being generally well informed about events around me, and virtually ceased all physical activity—believing any sports or entertainment was selfish and worldly. Cutting myself off socially from all but "the

Lord's people," I became extremely unbalanced, and a source of great concern to those who loved me.

I am now well aware that this was not at all what the Potter had in mind. He wants us to balance our spirituality with social graces, and keep us emotionally and physically fit and trim. This is all part of the finishing process. The Potter works with one hand inside the vessel and one hand outside, and He knows very well that this is the way to produce a balanced pot. As He gets a feel of us on the inside, He has a chance to detect a piece of grit or uneven lump, and deal with it. He knows the outside of the pot is not unimportant, for this will be the part that causes other pots to notice us in the first place, and mark the Master's finish on our lives; but He also knows that a pot is only going to be as good outside as it is inside! I have to work out for myself the difference between *balance* and *compromise* and trust Him to help me to do that by keeping me centered on Him.

And so, bathed in tears, centered on the wheel and balanced in His hands, the process continues. It is now time to be finished in the kiln. It is in the Potter's kiln that the greatest change takes place. Without the refining fire, the clay will dissolve the first time it is used to carry anything. Before the final firing, there will be the need for numerous other firings. Only the Potter knows how many of these there will be, and they will undoubtedly vary according to the coping capacity of each particular piece of art. But every vessel that is made will need to be toughened and proved by the pressure of intense heat. We can expect that there will be many and varied kiln experiences for all of us before we are through. Perhaps that is exactly where you are right now. Maybe you find yourself sitting in the kiln, being fired, and you are not enjoying it one little bit. It helps to realize that the Potter has not abandoned you but has actually allowed this to happen, and that this is simply part of the whole plan. It is in the kiln we learn some hard facts about ourselves, about others, and about our Divine Potter.

First of all, we learn that He has built in safeguards for the firing process. He has promised never to leave us in there, for example. The Master Potter keeps a watchful eye on the little pot through a peephole designed for that specific purpose. Having formed and fashioned us to His predetermined design, He knows exactly how much heat to allow, for He understands fully that the firing can cause a sag or slump in the clay. But isn't it hard when you are sitting there, and the heat is on, to believe He really does know what He is doing? Which of us has not demanded *out* as soon as He puts us *in?* Just as the clay needs to lie still to be bathed with water, so the vessel thus formed needs to sit still in the kiln, and stop hopping around, telling the Potter how long to bake him! I fully realize that that is a lot easier said than done!

And what about the kiln experience of watching someone you love being fired in the furnace? What mother has not tugged metaphorically at the Potter's robe, imploring Him on behalf of a suffering child to take the firey hot pot out before it crumbles away altogether? If we could only know for certain that the end result would be a happy one, we could perhaps bear the trauma better. It is at such times we must believe that:

The Expert Potter is *the* expert potter! He can gauge when we are finished perfectly, just from looking at us. He can tell by the color and the glow in our character, for it is the intense heat that causes the color to come up in the clay. That is the way, in fact, the Potter knows that that particular firing is finished.

I have seen the color come up in many a person's character, as they have been finished in the fire. I think of the time I sat by the bedside of a dear friend, as her doctor told her he had discovered a terminal malignancy. There were quiet questions and straight answers, and there were tears, and some apprehension, but, oh, the glow on the face of that woman! We who were to be her companions in the days that lay ahead witnessed a kaleidoscope of coping color that caught our breath and provoked our praise. I have seen the color and glow in another woman pot, who bore a long-awaited child and found him mongoloid!

I have witnessed the same glow in a little boy's face. I first met the little chap when he wouldn't come out of a cupboard in his house because his parents were getting a divorce! After he put his faith in the Potter, he not only emerged from his cupboard—he positively glowed with glee! His coping-carrying ability startled us all. The firing is supposed to cause character lines, not cracks in the pot's structure.

And then, in the end, there will be for all of us the final firing. We've talked a little about the vessel that refuses God's Son and resists the remodeling process—and is set forever in the sad shape of rejection. But for the one who does accept Christ, there will be a very different ending. The final firing will set us into the very shape of the Christ who lives within us. He is planning now to form us for that resurrection morning. When I awake, He promises that I shall be like Him—*baked* to break no more! It is in the final or *gloss* firing that the glaze is transformed into the shiny glasslike finish we admire in our favorite china. It is in the final fusion that the work is completed and most completely transformed. Pick up a piece of the finest bone china that you can find, and you will see that it is strangely and marvelously translucent. The light shines straight through it. So it will be in heaven. How hard it will be then, to remember that we started out as a limpid lump of clay.

The promise of the Potter is that through death the Christian will be so transformed he will be eternally durable, fitted for God's eternal shelf. He has promised a new and heavenly vessel in which we shall live forever, for He has told us that "if this earthly tabernacle be dissolved as if by fire, we know we have a house in heaven not made with hands!" (*See* 2 Corinthians 5:1.) Above all, we can know with a sure and settled assurance that when we are finally fired, we will never finally fail, for one day Christ shall be seen *through us,* and God will be glorified *in* us!

Have Thine own way, Lord,
  Have Thine own way!
Thou art the Potter;
  I am the clay.
Mold me and make me
  After Thy will,
While I am waiting,
  Yielded and still.

Have Thine own way, Lord,
   Have Thine own way!
Search me and try me,
   Master, to-day!
Whiter than snow, Lord,
   Wash me just now,
As in Thy presence
   Humbly I bow.

Have Thine own way, Lord,
   Have Thine own way!
Wounded and weary,
   Help me, I pray!
Power, all power,
   Surely is Thine!
Touch me and heal me,
   Saviour divine!

Have Thine own way, Lord,
   Have Thine own way!
Hold o'er my being
   Absolute sway.
Fill with Thy Spirit
   Till all shall see
Christ only, always,
   Living in me!

ADELAIDE A. POLLARD

WORKSHEET

Crumbling Clay

Suggested time—6 minutes

1. The Potter
   a) Review Psalms 119:73; Genesis 2:7; Zechariah 12:1.
   b) Read Psalm 139. Put the following verses in your own words: verses 13, 14, 15, 16.

Suggested time—6 minutes

2. The Clay
   a) What is God like?
      (Example: John 4:24   God is spiritual.)
      Psalms 90:2 _____.
      1 Corinthians 2:11 _____.
      John 11:35 _____.
   b) What do we mean when we say that man is made "in His image"?

Suggested time—10 minutes

3. Discuss: Do you have a problem with self-worth?
   a) What do you understand by:
      painted with the colors of your culture;
      shaped for the function of your future;
      handmade?
   b) How did the Potter shape the apostle Paul for his life's work? (Philippians 3:4–6).

Suggested time—10-15 minutes

4. Review the following illustrative pictures and share a personal application of one of them. (*Keep short.*)
   (Example: God made me "pliable" through grief, when He took my husband home this year.)

    a) Wet clay
    b) Centered on the wheel
    c) Balanced—one hand inside—one hand outside
    d) Firing in the kiln
       timing
       transparency

Suggested time—10 minutes

5. The Promise of the Potter: Vessels of Glory
   Look up the following verses:
    a) 2 Corinthians 5:1, 2
    b) Psalms 17:15
    c) 1 John 3:2
    d) Romans 9:22–24
    e) Romans 8:29
    f) Psalms 16:11

Suggested time—5 minutes

6. Prayer Time

4

Disobedient Disciples

Now the word of the Lord came unto Jonah the son of Amittai, saying,

Arise, go to Nineveh, that great city, and cry against it; for their wickedness is come up before me.

But Jonah rose up to flee unto Tarshish from the presence of the Lord, and went down to Joppa; and he found a ship going to Tarshish: so he paid the fare thereof, and went down into it, to go with them unto Tarshish from the presence of the Lord.

Jonah 1:1–3

A story of some small fry chased by a big fish.

God's ultimate purpose for mankind is that "every knee shall bow to Him, and every tongue confess that Jesus Christ is Lord to the glory of God the Father" (*see* Philippians 2:10, 11). But God's world is in a mess! Men live and die without God, without Christ, and without hope. The means by which God's message of salvation is to be conveyed to the mess is by the men who receive it themselves, and pass the good news on to others. But this is where we have a problem. Jesus taught His disciples to pray that God's will would be done on earth, as it is done in heaven. The story of Jonah graphically illustrates that the will of God is not something that the men of God always do.

It would all be so much easier if God didn't have to use people. We see in this story that the Lord had very little trouble sending a "great wind" and stirring up some "great waves," but winds and waves can't preach. It was when He appointed a red-blooded prophet with a mind of his own that the fun began. Jonah did not want to do the will of God and take the Word of God to the world of God.

If we have a problem, we would usually give anything to simply snap our fingers and have it disappear. God, however, is not like us, and for that we should be truly grateful. If God snapped His fingers so His problems disappeared, *we* would disappear, because we are His problems. But God's ways are higher than our ways and His thoughts deeper than our thoughts, and we find that He patiently works His problems out.

The story of Jonah reveals God's patient and tender concern, not only for the lost inhabitants of Nineveh, but for His stubborn rebellious prophet as well.

Not long ago my husband came home totally exhausted from a series of very demanding lectures. He was faced with a pile of mail, inviting him to go to the four corners of the earth and preach more sermons. Glancing through the pile of letters, he sighed and commented, "Just occasionally, I'm tempted to feel like a sermon machine." I knew exactly what he meant. I, too, have felt a little like that in a much lesser degree. But we have both learned one fact, and that is that God does not look upon us as sermon machines. He cares about us as people, not just as prophets. He loves us, and seeing our tears shows us His concern when we're just plain pooped out.

Now that's the first thing I want to talk about. I have discovered the "pooped prophet" malady to be quite common amongst God's servants. Many of the Lord's people are tired out. They can be tired of many things. They may be tired of going to meetings, tired of singing hymns, teaching a Sunday-school class, serving on committees, or just plain tired of other Christians. I am encouraged to see God's sweet caring for Jonah in this regard. The Ninevites are mentioned in passing, but it is *Jonah* that God is ministering to. This does not mean that He does not care about the heathen—of course, He does, *but* He does not cease to care for His own, as they care for the heathen *He cares for!*

I think of another illustration of a pooped prophet in the Scriptures: that of Elijah in 1 Kings, chapter 19. He had been running the race that was set before him at such a spanking pace, that he had just passed out at the finishing line. Lying face down in the dust, he requested that he might die. Again, I am touched by the tender understanding of God. He came not with words of rebuke but with gentle reminders of His love. He did not say, "You stupid, sinful, backslidden, pathetic prophet—shape up or ship out!" but rather roused him from his deep despondency with these very practical words of encouragement through His angel: ". . . Arise and eat; because the journey is too great for thee" (verse 7).

I can remember "touches of the Trinity" like that. There have been tired nights, when I have lost my perspective of God, envisaging Him in the most distorted way. It is at those times I have imagined Him standing over my exhausted, crumpled body with a big, beating stick with the word MINISTRY written on it. What a relief to realize He is saying to me, "Jill, arise and eat—the journey is too great for thee." Then, like Elijah, I have been able to walk the extra mile in the strength of *that* nourishment. He knows our frame, you see, and remembers that we are dust! If we are not careful, we can get to the point of feeling guilty about any rest or relaxation we take at all.

Not long ago, someone asked me what I did for relaxation. "I jog," I replied. "Oh," said the lady. "That's wonderful. Could I ask what you think about as you jog? Do you memorize the Scriptures, pray for the needs of the world, or wrestle with some deep theological problem?" I have to admit she looked a little startled (and certainly a mite disappointed), when I answered, "Quite frankly, I am thinking, *One more tree! Just one more tree!*" It was not all that long ago that I came to understand I did not *have* to turn everything into a spiritual exercise. If God counts rest and relaxation a valid necessity for the Jonahs and Elijahs of this world, then He certainly counts it so for us lesser mortals. He did not tell Elijah to "arise and pray," or "arise and study," or even "arise and share the four spiritual laws with Jezebel!" He told him to "arise and *eat.*" What fun! But then fun is valid too. Did you learn that yet—little pooped prophet—whoever you are?

But maybe the problems we give God are not because we are pooped, but because we are prejudiced. Jonah was a true-blue Jew. Yes, he was, and he didn't really dig anyone who wasn't. He certainly had no brief for the Ninevites, that is for sure. He was suffering from a severe case of love lack, a damaging deficiency of devotion. Now this is a very serious ailment. It is a sure-fire way of making certain the *Word* of God doesn't get to the *world* of God, that the *will* of God might be done. Many times God cannot use us because of our loveless lives. I am often asked to address students on Christian campuses about their desires to be missionaries. I ask them a very elementary question. It has nothing to do with grades, courses, or anything like that. I simply ask them, "How do you get on with people you don't like?" Oftentimes, if they are honest, they may tell me they are getting a *D* in that, but *A*'s in Bible.

Then I ask them gently how ever they imagine they will love people somewhere else, if they cannot handle their interaction with them here? The mission field is populated with the same awkward characters we have as our neighbors at home. The church abroad may be comprised of many more weird and woolly believers than the fellowship we meet with in our native land. In other words, we'll never flame abroad until we flicker at home! The miracle of the Book of Jonah is not the fact that the big fish arrived at the right moment, under the right boat in the right storm, with the right appetite, but rather that the right changes took place in the heart and life of Jonah. The greatest miracle of all is to see love produced in a prejudiced heart. Only God can do that, of course. But He is committed to the task. He promises to give us "a heart of flesh for our heart of stone" (*see* Ezekiel 36:26).

This is one of God's biggest problems, because it *demands* our *cooperation.* We are back once again to the question of the will of God conflicting with the will of man. So many times we just do not want to love. Like Jonah, God tells us to go to Nineveh, and we take off to Tarshish (a town incidentally at the opposite end of the country). There have been many Ninevehs in my life. I can remember God telling me to go and preach to the street kids. I didn't want to go. Then I can recollect God telling me to minister to women. This I most *certainly* did not want to do! However, I decided it would be expedient to do it anyway, because I didn't want God to send a submarine after me like He did after Jonah!

Accepting the invitations I received to travel and to speak, I was coldly obedient but people got saved. Women repented. The more I spoke, the more they wanted, and the angrier I got! Then one day a dear friend sat me down and told me that I was pretty good at lecturing—but pretty poor at loving. "You do not love these women," she said. She was right, and what was more, I had no intention of doing so. *Why, I reasoned, if I did, who knew where I would end up?* Probably I would find myself on the women's speaking circuit buried in women. No, thanks! But I found out that God won't let us pout about. He insists on loving us too much to let us live that way. He refuses to allow us to sleep our way through the storm. Like Jonah, He sends all sorts of people to shake us awake and will not allow us to get away with our prejudices or sink into passivity. The ship's captain came to Jonah, as he snoozed his way through the crisis he himself had caused, and said to him:

... What meanest thou, O sleeper? arise, call upon thy God....

Jonah 1:6

God uses all sorts and conditions of men to wake us up. He may even shame us through an unbeliever who's doing more praying than we are. I am sure Jonah was shamed when he woke up to the fact that those heathen sailors were calling upon their gods, while he was sleeping through the storm. I thank God for my friend who like that ship's captain, shook me awake to the realization that I had made a willful decision *not* to love, and needed to repent of that sinful choice.

We are told that we have an energy crisis in our country. The government is desperately concerned about it. It knows, however, that its concern alone will not solve the problem. It needs the cooperation of the population. I heard a well-known professor of political science make the comment that the problem lies in the attitude of our "me now" generation, and that individual apathy must go. He declared that the cumulative effect of this individual apathy will lead to an energy disaster. "This is a huge danger to our world," he said. He told of a test he had set for his students. He had asked them this question: "Which is the biggest problem concerning the energy shortage: ignorance or apathy?" One of his best students replied, "I don't know and I don't care!" Funny, yes! But that's convicting, too, because some of God's "best students," if honest, would have to answer the same way. They are experiencing their own spiritual-

energy crisis, sleeping, whilst the storm storms; being insensitive to
the needs around them; and are living lives of lethal lethargy. We
are told that 2.8 billion people in the world today have never heard
the Gospel of Jesus Christ. Now *that's* a storm! What does that do to
us? If we love at all, it will involve more than a few snores in response.

Because God loves us far too much to let us get away with our "I
don't know and I don't care" attitudes, we can be sure He will
eventually chase us down. There was one fact that Jonah quickly
learned: the futile occupation of running away from the will of God.
However hard he ran, God had longer legs than he had, and was
intent on chasing him back into blessing. God will find a way,
sometimes a commonplace, and occasionally an uncommonplace
way to restrict our movements, so that we have to confront the
issue. He may, as He did with Jacob, put our thigh out of joint, as
He wrestles with us; or then again He may throw us together in
some solitary situation with a Christian roommate, as He did with
Onesimus, the runaway slave, who escaped from his Christian master, only to end up in a prison cell with Paul! (*See* the Epistle to
Philemon.) He uses many a big fish to carry us small fry back to
where we belong. There have been times He has shut me up within
the whale of ill health, and the world has said, "*Laid aside by illness*"; but I have come to recognize His hand in it, and known instead that I have been "called aside for stillness." It has been during
such days that the doctors have worked on my body, while God has
worked on my soul.

Which of us cannot but sympathize with Jonah's statement "I
cried *by reason of mine affliction . . .* " (Jonah 2:2 *italics mine).* For
some of us problem prophets, it takes either restriction or affliction
to cause us to cry to the Lord again. As the story of the making of
this man of God progresses, we begin to see that restriction and affliction led to conviction:

> . . . I cried by reason of mine affliction unto the Lord, and he heard
> me; out of the belly of hell cried I, and thou heardest my voice. For
> thou hadst cast me into the deep, in the midst of the seas; and the

floods compassed me about: all thy billows and thy waves passed over me. Then I said, I am cast out of thy sight; yet I will look again toward thy holy temple. . . .When my soul fainted within me, I remembered the Lord. . . .

Jonah 2:2–4, 7

Words from seven different psalms litter the second chapter of Jonah. God's Word had begun to get through to God's worker. There is one thing for sure, and that is that the Word of God will not get to the world of God until it first gets to us. Convinced of Jonah's repentance, God spoke to the fish "and it vomited out Jonah upon the dry land" (2:10).

So far so good. Picking himself up, Jonah set off toward Nineveh, for the Word of the Lord came to Jonah "the second time" (3:1). "Arise, go unto Nineveh, that great city, and preach unto it the preaching that I bid thee" (verse 2). You would have thought after Jonah's unbelievable experience in the fish's stomach that this would have been the end of the story. But it isn't. Jonah is certainly seen to be obedient, as he marches briskly through Nineveh "paying his vows" (2:9) and preaching the words God had bidden him to preach to the Ninevites; but the God of grace had not changed His mind about reaching and teaching the preacher as well. His purpose and plans for His problem prophet had not yet been accomplished. There had certainly been progress, but after all the dust had settled, God still found He had a mad messenger on His hands! The people of Nineveh had responded in an unprecedented way to Jonah's ministry. The results and statistics were staggering. Even the cows were decked out in sackcloth and ashes (3:8). But remember again the concern of the Saviour is not for statistics. People are not numbers to God. He is interested in the individual, and concerned with what we *are* more than *what we do*. It was time to work a miracle in His prophet's heart. He decided if Jonah was going to continue to behave like a child, He would have to treat him like a child and tell him a story. He would use a picture to perfect His prophet—a parable, in fact.

So Jonah went out of the city, and sat on the east side of the city, and there made him a booth, and sat under it in the shadow, till he might see what would become of the city.

And the Lord God prepared a gourd, and made it to come up over Jonah, that it might be a shadow over his head, to deliver him from his grief. So Jonah was exceedingly glad of the gourd.

But God prepared a worm when the morning rose the next day, and it smote the gourd, that it withered.

4:5–7

This is where the worm comes in. Think, if you will, about Jonah, sitting in the shade of the vine that God had caused to miraculously grow up over his head in the night to shade him. The next day, without warning, the pleasant plant began to wither. How could this be? As Jonah watched, he saw a rather sick-looking worm wriggling unsteadily out from under the foliage, and setting off in a northeasterly direction. Whether God told Jonah that He had appointed the little worm, or the prophet figured it all out for himself, we will never know. We do know, however, that writing about the little creature, Jonah said, "And God prepared a worm," so we understand that by the time the tale was told, Jonah believed in the worm's calling! Yes, that's right, I said *calling*, for the Bible says, "God 'prepared' a worm" (verse 7). Some time ago, as I struggled to prepare a message for a group of missionaries, my eyes fell upon that particular verse. What a text for a lot of pressured, pooped servants of God! I knew men and women were coming to that convention leveled by their work loads, looking for help. Well, I could tell them that "God prepared a worm." They appreciated the thought. As Jonah watched the little worm work, I think he began to get the message, too.

Animals and insects have often been used to teach mere mortal men a few things. I think of Scotland's Robert Bruce, who sat in a highland cave, totally discouraged. He was debating his strategy in the struggle against the foe (which happened to be the English!). As he thought through his plans, his attention was caught by a spider trying to spin a web. Time after time, the little thing would swing out on its silver thread, struggling to find something somewhere to attach it to. Time after time, it failed—only to try again. Robert Bruce got the message. He would try again and again and again, until Scotland won! Imagine Jonah sitting under his plant in the hot sun, wrestling with his problem. Then think of him watching the little worm that God had appointed—a worm who chose to be obedient, when that could not have been an easy thing for it to do. (Look at it from the worm's vantage point.)

Even though the insect must surely have felt good about being elected to help out (for it wasn't every day that God appointed a worm), it was still a miracle that it obeyed. Even though it knew that God must believe in it, it still must have been hard to believe in itself. Anyway, the creature had obviously been thrilled to be selected and enjoyed a sense of security. The early birds kept missing their shot, as he wriggled along the ground frighteningly visible and vulnerable. To know you have been selected and protected makes you feel—well, no more than a worm—but a worthy worm, at least. For the worm to know that he had been born for "such a time as this" must have created a great sense of value within him. Little is big then, you know.

Watching the worm, Jonah must have relented. There was no doubt about it, he had begun to feel like a worm. I don't think he liked himself very much at that moment. You usually don't, when you are mad at the world in general and at God in particular. He was not the first (and neither will he be the last) to come to such a devastating self discovery. Until now, Jonah had had no trouble at all believing that the Ninevites were a bunch of the worst sort of worms there happened to be, but at last, he began to see that it was only a case of variety; and, slowly, a sense of his own worminess in the sight of *God* pervaded his soul. Perhaps he started to understand Bildad the Shuhite's final speech from the Book of Job when he asked, "How then can a man be righteous before God? How can one born of woman be pure? If even the moon is not bright and the stars are not pure in his eyes, how much less man, who is but a maggot—a son of man, who is only a worm!" (Job 25:4–6 NIV) or David's inspired cry, "But I am a worm, and no man . . ." (Psalms

22:6). It is hard to imagine a lower form of animal life than the worm, and yet graced by the Godhead and appointed by the Almighty, worms can rise to heights only God can imagine for them. In the end, we are all leveled to be lifted—reduced to be enlarged. Jonah's anger directed at everyone and everything else in sight, was in all probability a deflected emotion. He was probably essentially angry at his own wormlike attitude. The little worm had been "heart-wormingly" obedient, and Jonah was touched, for its response to its Creator had gone above and beyond the call of duty.

Just imagine, after being selected and protected, to find yourself in the place of service assigned to you, and hear the amazing heavenly commission: "Go and eat a cacti" [or a vine, if you like!]. I mean *worms,* don't you know? *Worms,* can't you see? And what's more, worms don't *want to* either, and even if they did, a six-foot-tall cactus is a tall order. The whole thing was quite ridiculous. But then God's assignments usually are. The task is *huge.* Two billion people who have never heard of Christ? Just how do you sink your spiritual teeth into that one? *Go to Nineveh,* when you are a true-blue Jew and love only those you like? *Impossible.* You can be all elected, protected, and yet end up being dejected about the whole selected project.

Poor little worm, Jonah must have thought. Fancy finding himself setting off at a grand lick in the general direction of the desert, spurred on by this weird, driving sensation that he had never experienced before—one that made him strangely cacti-hungry; and then to arrive and find himself facing a task like this! Not only did the little worm have to eat a cactus, he had to eat it under Jonah's malevolent eye.

As the worm started to work, he must have felt pretty sick as well, but then who says you'll always feel *good* doing the will of God? The whale hadn't—obedience had made him ill, too, you remember. There is the strangest philosophy abroad in Christian circles today that if you do the will of God, you will feel good doing it; become a success, and grow rich in the process. In my limited experience, I have found that to do the will of God will sometimes mean you are lonely, occasionally mean you get hurt, or may even end up making you thoroughly sick! For some people, it has even meant death. No, it is not always an easy or pleasant thing to do the will of God. But let me hasten to add, there is undoubtedly joy after the doing. ". . . Jesus . . . for the joy that was set before him endured the cross, despising the shame, and is set down at the right hand of the throne of God" (Hebrews 12:2). The joy awaited Him at the right hand of God. It was set before Him *after* the cross and the shame, not before, and not during it. There is not much joy in being crucified, I can assure you. There was not much joy in the whale or the worm's stomach either, but once it was over—what a relief! The joy of knowing that we do His will is usually a retrospective happiness.

After a night out on the streets of Europe, sharing Christ with youngsters who really didn't want to listen, I would be filled with an incredible sense of completion—*after* the cross and *after* the shame —always *after.* Jonah had certainly not enjoyed his week's ministry in Nineveh. He had preached short sermons, walked on briskly, and couldn't wait to have it over with, and get out of the place. But now, on the hillside, one of the most honest prayers of the Bible was prayed: ". . . take . . . my life from me . . ." (4:3). (Prayer has been described as "the debating chamber of the soul." It is the arena of argument where God has a chance to win the debate.) After submission to His will, the peace that passes understanding will pervade us; and *love* will leap the limits of our prejudice and pique. We know God had His way in Jonah's life in the end, because Jonah wrote the book and told us all about it. He wanted to help us to learn from his mistakes.

I like to think of the prophet Jonah in heaven, happy at last, surrounded by his Ninevites—jewels in his crown. I also like to think of the little glorified worm sitting in heaven too. (Though, of course, I have no Scripture backing for such an assumption.) Somehow, I think he might be there anyway, and if he is, I want to thank him for being such a great example to me.

So often I have come to the end of some Christian commitments and end up with that awful "worm and no man" feeling. There's nothing quite like it. At such times, the world doesn't fade away. The multitudes still clamor for attention; the children are crying;

the sick ones are dying; and ignorance devours the minds of men. Apathy lives and breeds indolence and worse. The cacti seem so *huge,* and I feel so very, very *small.* Just where do I begin? It is at such deep, dark points I think of the little worm, and then I know the answer. I can start like he did, with the first bite. After that I will know it can be done. The second bite will become a grand possibility, and the third one a cinch—and on and on I will go—until the plant withers and the thing is done. Sick though I may be, God will be pleased and so will I, for oh, joy, I will not have disappointed Him!

Jesus, Fountain of my days,
   Well-spring of my heart's delight,
Brightness of my morning rays,
   Solace of my hours of night;
When I see Thee, I arise
To the hope of cloudless skies.

Oh how weary were the years
   Ere Thy form to me was known;
Oh how gloomy were the fears
   When I seemed to be alone;
I despaired the storm to brave
Till Thy footprints touched the wave.

But Thy presence on the deep
   Calmed the pulses of the sea,
And the waters sank to sleep
   In the rest of seeing Thee;
And my once rebellious will
Heard the mandate, Peace be still!

Now Thy will and mine are one,
   Heart in heart, and hand in hand;
All the clouds have touched the sun,
   And the ships have reached the land;
For Thy love has said to me,
No more night! and no more sea!

GEORGE MATHESON

WORKSHEET

Disobedient Disciples

Suggested time—10 minutes

Discussion:

1. Identify your Nineveh—and the reasons you are heading for Tarshish. Are you pooped, prejudiced, pouting, or passive?

Suggested time—6 minutes

2. We will never be able to obey God if we do not know what He is telling us to do. We need to be observing the commands in the Scriptures. Example: Read 1 Thessalonians 5 with a partner, and make a list of all the commands you find there. Try to obey one or two of them this week. (Remember we need to take these steps in "bite-sized pieces.")

Suggested time—6 minutes

3. Give an example of the way God has restricted you in some way, in order to talk to you.

Suggested time—5 minutes

4. Look up these verses: Job 25:4–6 and Psalms 22:6.
   Can you identify with the worm? Why?

Suggested time—2 minutes

5. How do we know Jonah allowed God to change him?

Suggested time—10 minutes

6. Jonah failed; then Jonah succeeded. Think of five ways God worked in his life to make that happen. (Particularly note chapter 5 of Jonah.)

Suggested time—6 minutes

7. Do you think Jonah obeyed because he was motivated by fear? If
   so, do you think this was a worthy motivation? If fear can help us
   overcome failure, could it be a good reaction? (Read Proverbs
   8:13.)

Suggested time—5 minutes

8. Prayer Time
   a) Make sure you tell God how you *really* feel, just like Jonah
      did. Let God tell you how He really feels, too.
   b) Pray for Nineveh.
   c) Pray for God's prophets.

5

Brittle Bones

The hand of the Lord was upon me, and carried me out in the spirit of the Lord, and set me down in the midst of the valley which was full of bones,

And caused me to pass by them round about: and, behold, there were very many in the open valley; and, lo, they were very dry.

And he said unto me, Son of man, can these bones live? And I answered, O Lord God, thou knowest.

Again he said unto me, Prophesy upon these bones, and say unto them, O ye dry bones, hear the word of the Lord.

Thus saith the Lord God unto these bones; Behold, I will cause breath to enter into you, and ye shall live:

And I will lay sinews upon you, and will bring up flesh upon you, and cover you with skin, and put breath in you, and ye shall live; and ye shall know that I am the Lord.

So I prophesied as I was commanded: and as I prophesied, there was a noise, and behold a shaking, and the bones came together, bone to his bone.

And when I beheld, lo, the sinews and the flesh came up upon them, and the skin covered them above: but there was no breath in them.

Then said he unto me, Prophesy unto the wind, prophesy, son of man, and say to the wind, Thus saith the Lord God; Come from the four winds, O breath, and breathe upon these slain, that they may live.

So I prophesied as he commanded me, and the breath came into them, and they lived, and stood up upon their feet, an exceeding great army.

Then he said unto me, Son of man, these bones are the whole house of Israel: behold, they say, our bones are dried, and our hope is lost: we are cut off for our parts.

Therefore prophesy and say unto them, Thus saith the Lord God; Behold, O my people, I will open your graves, and cause you to come up out of your graves, and bring you into the land of Israel.

Ezekiel 37:1–12

The "grave" story of born-again bones, skeletal staff, and rattling religiosity.

Burned bones, lying in a hot spot of their own making, with apparently no solid frame of reference, lay shimmering in the heat. They represented the whole house of Israel. The Bone Maker "Whose hands had fashioned them together round about, clothing them with skin and flesh, and knitting them together with sinews— had granted them life, shown them kindness, and watched over their spirit" (*see* Job 10:11, 12). He certainly intended them to be up on their feet and ready to go, a functioning part of His "exceeding great army"! God's desire for all of His soldiers is a high state of combat fitness. There is a war to be won, and He has raised the standard and set the battle in array. We sing hymns about it, like the one that says:

> Fight the good fight
> With all thy might.

This *good* fight is the conflict between good and evil, and those of us who know God are supposed to be out there in the thick of things. How is it then, that today many born-again bones are lying around in visionless valleys, mere shadows of all they were meant to be? How can we explain the fact that spooky saints are haunting our churches, frightening away the curious inquirer with their rattling religiosity? If we were ever to doubt God's thoughts concerning this matter, we have only to listen to the urgent language of the text:

". . . I will make breath to enter you, and you will come to life" (Ezekiel 37:5 NIV). God undoubtedly has the blessing of the bones in mind. Now if we want to find out, "What were the bare bones of this matter?" we have to ask ourselves, "What was the matter with the bones?"

Our text gives the answer. First of all they were very *dry.* "Our bones are dried up," they said. Second, they were very *depressed* because they were very dry. "Our hope is gone; we are cut off," they complained (verse 11). This dusty depression had given them a sad sense of isolation. Even though they found themselves in the midst of a whole valley full of bones, they still felt pretty *desolate.*

You see, we must never confuse numbers with blessing. A South American evangelist told a convention that at one point in his ministry he had become very self-satisfied. His church was growing, and more and more people were becoming involved in the activities; but without realizing it, he had begun to confuse *numbers* with *blessing.* The situation was very *deceiving.* Then one day, as he was driving home, he passed the town cemetery and noticed that that was growing too. He began asking himself some hard questions. He wondered if his big, bustling church was simply a brimming bone yard, and decided that from that point on, he would not confuse numbers with blessing.

We must not confuse *busy-ness* with blessing either. There may be busy little Bible-believing bones, gyrating all over our churches; but as far as seeing active duty and fighting in the ranks of God's exceeding great army, they would have to admit, if honest, that they have been absent without leave, lying around bone idle, wasting away time, talents, and opportunities for far too long. If this is the case with our particular fellowship, then this is indeed a grave matter.

It isn't a question of how many committed committees we have operating, but rather how many committed Christians we are producing. Are we so busy planning church picnics, women's day outings, or arguing about the color of the new church carpet, we have little time or energy left to teach our people how to pray and study the Bible? Are we running around in evangelical circles, thinking up new ideas for popular programs that will entertain our people (and keep them coming), or are we motivating folk to minister and serve one another? Do we want to keep people happy or make people holy? This is not to say that holiness is not happiness, for holy means *whole*—full, fat, and satisfied.

You see once we become a born-again bone, that is only the beginning. Sinews and flesh are supposed to give substance to our spiritual frame. My dictionary defines a skeleton as a permanent nucleus, ready for filling up with vegetable matter. As we responsibly do our part, eating the spiritual food that God has prepared for us, then we will begin to shape up. The valley of vision thus becomes a place of choice for those of us who profess to know the Bone Maker and claim to have received His life. But it is this very matter of freedom of choice that is the problem, for it is at this point the *will of God* meets the *won't of man.* "*Why* will ye die?" Jehovah inquires of Israel, as they wasted away to nothing. "We pine away because of our transgressions and our sins" they replied somewhat honestly (*see* 33:10, 11). Having willfully neglected their relationship with God and with His Word, Israel admitted to the fact that they were suffering from a chronic case of spiritual malnutrition.

It is a sin to willfully refuse the divinity's diet He so graciously provides. God sets our spiritual table Sunday by Sunday, and He also lays it daily in the dining room of our soul, so it should come as no surprise to hear Him ask, as He asked the house of Israel, "Why will ye die?"

Have you ever heard of *anorexia nervosa?* This is an illness described in *The Golden Cage* by Sir William Gull, a British physician, as a "disease of the rich and privileged—a nervous consumption." He describes the victim as "a skeleton only clad with skin and the chief symptom that of severe starvation leading to a devastating weight loss—and this in the midst of plenty! The outstanding feature of this problem is a 'relentless pursuit of excessive thinness on behalf of the patient.' Anorexics are defiant and stubborn people," Gull writes.

There was a time in my life when I lived within a mile of a Bible school. Week after week, men of God took the Word of God and explained it to the students. I was free to have it all explained to me, as well, as my husband was on staff at the school. It was a case of feast or famine. Being in a stubborn and rebellious mood, I chose famine. Pursuing excessive thinness, I developed a chronic case of spiritual anorexia. Now remember that this is a disease of the wealthy and privileged, and even though God had shown me kindness, watched over my spirit, and prepared a banquet of rich, spiritual fare, well within reach, I deliberately lay down to die in a desert of my own making. It was not a wilderness of inactivity either, for while I was losing weight, I was working out. I was busy but bony. The frightening thing about anorexia is the *mind-set* that one cultivates. To stubbornly refuse nourishing food, for whatever reason, is a totally self-destructive course, and one you would think would be too painful to pursue. In the end, it takes a radical change of mind to turn the corner and choose to be a healthy, whole person, instead of a bag of bones. I guess I just got tired of being chronically hungry—and *that* in the midst of plenty—and decided at last to swap busy-ness for blessedness.

Now it is time to introduce Ezekiel, a man who was certainly not the skeletal sort of saint that we have been talking about. Somewhere along the line he had been *captured,* choosing to let the Bone Maker get a good grip upon his life, for he tells us, "The hand of the Lord was upon me" (verse 1). (That phrase reminds me of my homeland and the famous "British Bobbie"—the term we use for our English policemen. Those gentlemen do not carry guns, but rather have for their help, heavy rubber truncheons. They sport whistles, used to summon assistance, and they all develop very long arms! Whenever an arrest is made, that "long arm of the law" stretches out, as the officer grips the culprit's shoulder. Then, with all the authority invested in them, the policemen inform the offenders that they have been apprehended in the name of the law.) It is after this manner that Ezekiel describes his own divine arrest. He had not been forced at gunpoint to comply with some heavy heavenly demand, but rather found himself choosing to go quietly and pay his dues, so fingered by the Divine and gripped by the Godhead, was he. Once grasped, he was well on the way to grasping for himself the reason for which he had been grasped by God in the first place. He would get to know God; he would feast at His table; he would be obedient to His call.

Having been *captured* by the Lord, he was next *carried* by the Spirit into the middle of the valley of dry bones. I am sure if Ezekiel had been consulted, there were many other places of service that he would have suggested to the Almighty—those that he felt would have been far more appropriate—but he hadn't been consulted, he had been carried. This is usually the case.

At this point, of course, he could well have decided to join the heap, rather than be the helper to the heap he had been sent to be. I, too, have found myself in certain situations and have decided too quickly to ask for a transfer. I cannot remember being consulted either—just carried.

There is one particular dry and dusty valley in England that comes to mind. We were living in the country at the time, and no one seemed to go to church anymore. The church buildings were very pretty, but what good was that when they were pretty empty? Here and there a few old bones nodded in the pews. Most of my neighbors were aged, whilst I was young. I felt very much like Ezekiel must have felt when he heard the Lord say, "Preach to the bones!"

As I prayed about it, I seemed to hear Him tell me:

> Bone again bone
> Clothed and complete
> Nourished by God
> Standing on your feet
> Gripped by Jehovah
> And carried at His will
> Into dusty deadness
> Blessing to instill—!

I thought of the question He had asked Ezekiel: "Son of man, can these bones live?" and, like Ezekiel, I couldn't help but answer, "Lord, Thou alone knowest." Somehow I didn't believe that they could. Not *these* bones! My neighbors were a generation away from regular church attendance. The local pastors had lost heart, and who could blame them? I well remember a wizened little old lady telling me a new preacher had come to their congregation. She didn't know what to make of him. "If you ask me, he's a bit too religious," she commented wryly. I perked up my ears at that, because he didn't sound like the last two preachers, who, quite frankly, hadn't been religious at all. I found out to my delight that this particular young man was a born-again bone who had been *captured* by the Lord, and *carried* by the Spirit, and set down right in our midst. I was so excited. Now surely God would bring some life into our valley. But the young pastor grew discouraged, and soon became part of the heap. A short time after he had arrived, he left, and I realized anew that this was a desolate place, indeed. But I *couldn't* leave. This was our home. This was our village and these were *my bones.* The first step to the blessing of the bones was the belief that God had carried me by His Spirit into that particular valley; set me down "in the midst" of them, and commanded me (and nobody else but me) to "preach to them." Stuart was away most of the time, and so he couldn't do it, and the preacher had left because he would *not* do it—and that left me. I realized that the blessing of the bones would have to begin with my own blessing.

In fact, the whole thing becomes a matter of obedience, for after you've been *captured* and *carried,* you find yourself *commanded* to preach, just as Ezekiel had been. Some do it better than others, of course, for spiritual gift is involved, but all of us can pass on a message to a *bone.* The word *preach* means to "tell forth plainly," and anyone can do that—with practice. All we have to do is to find out just what it is we are supposed to say and say it. We needn't worry about that either, as God told Ezekiel *exactly* what He wanted him to say, and His methods haven't changed. God promises to inspire us, and also to look after the results. He does not tell us to get down on our hands and knees and rattle the bones into shape. He commands us simply to listen to His Word and communicate it. I thought about the young pastor with his "skeleton staff" that had come to that difficult place to serve a handful of people, and I wished, oh, how I wished that he had stayed around long enough to see the miracle happen! For after a time, there was a shaking and a moving in our valley, and the bones began to stand up. The five little old ladies in my Bible class became eighty little ladies—and what's more, they were no longer famished, but fat! They marched around bearing witness to God's resurrection power. One shared with a terminally ill friend how Christ had taken away her fear of death. The sick neighbor caught her hand and asked her to read her some words of comfort. Turning to the Bible lesson of the week, she read to her the words from 2 Corinthians 5 that said:

> Now we know that if the earthly tent we live in is destroyed, we have a building from God, an eternal house in heaven, not built by human hands. Meanwhile we groan, longing to be clothed with our heavenly dwelling, because when we are clothed, we will not be found naked. For while we are in this tent, we groan and are burdened, because we do not wish to be unclothed but to be clothed with our heavenly dwelling, so that what is mortal may be swallowed up by life. Now it is God who has made us for this very purpose and has given us the Spirit as a deposit, guaranteeing what is to come.
>
> 2 Corinthians 5:1–5 NIV

The sick lady smiled. The tent of her body was indeed being dismantled, but now she understood that God had provided a permanent residence in heaven and was waiting to clothe her spirit with it. She couldn't get out of her bed to come to the meetings in my home, but she knew three or four of her friends she could call and encourage to attend. Over the months that followed, the women shared their new experiences with anyone that would listen, and it wasn't long until the sound of an awakening was heard in our valley. I have often had the experience of being told by the organizing committee of evangelistic meetings that "this city is a very, very dead place; it is desolate," they say. "Great," I reply. "Let's go and preach to the bones!"

When Stuart was invited to accept a call to pastor a church in Milwaukee, he was told, "Don't go there. That town has been a graveyard of evangelism for years." I saw my husband's eyes light up, as he thought about his God of life and resurrection power who specializes in graveyards. He also knew that God uses blessing bones to make things happen. It's a question of letting Him *capture* us, then *carry* us, and then *command* us to preach to the bones.

Where are you serving God just now? Are you dry and depressed, desolate or dead? Has your confidence gone? Are you feeling cut off from the Bone Maker and other born-again bones around you? Perhaps you are dryer than you've ever been in the whole of your spiritual life. Why not let His hand grip you anew, and consider again the call that carried you there in the first place. Ask yourself just what it was that He commanded you to do? What was the message that He asked you to preach? Have you resorted to entertainment, or some modern manipulative method to set the fractured fragments into place? What fake finagling are you trying, to get at least a slight rattle from the rows of ribs that face you Sunday by sad Sunday? Why not start again, and ask Him what it is He wants you both to do and to say? "But I've tried that," you say, "and nothing happened—nothing stirred." Then perhaps you forgot to pray (Ezekiel 37:9). Ezekiel was not only commanded to preach; he was also commanded to pray. "Prophesy unto the wind, prophesy, son of man, and say to the wind, Thus saith the Lord God; Come from the four winds, O breath, and breathe upon these slain, that they may live" (verse 9). "So," said Ezekiel, "I prophesied as he commanded me, and the breath came into them . . ." (verse 10).

In the end, we will have to learn to call upon the Spirit. We can stick it out in dry desperation. We can preach faithfully week after week, and even see the sinews and the flesh begin to fill in the frames of our people. We can certainly begin to feed them faithfully, but in the end, we will need to know what it is to pray with power.

If we are to see the miracle of all miracles take place, there will be one or two things that will have to happen before the wind blows. There will be a certain responsibility that we will have to undertake before we can call on God to breathe upon our dull despair and set us free. The responsibility we have is to respond to the preaching. It was, after all, in response to the preaching of God's Word that the bones came together. *So I prophesied as I was commanded: and as I [preached], there was a noise, and behold a shaking,* and *the bones came together, bone to his bone* (verse 7). (Notice that there was noise coming from the bones, as well as from the preacher!)

When God begins to work, the preacher will be the first one that God rattles. As we respond in obedience we earn the right to apply the Word to others. Our ministry will then prove to be a moving thing indeed. The bones will come together. Do you remember the complaint of the little bones, as they lay in their desperate condition? "We are cut off," they cried. Feeling unconnected with God and with each other, they confessed that sins and offenses had come in between. An offense is the act of hurting someone else. Have we offended another? Have we been contentious? Did we pick a fight? Do we know that it is a bone of contention with God when *we* are a bone of contention? God doesn't like some of the things that we've done and said, and if at all possible, He wants us to come together bone to bone, to say that we are sorry, and to start again. He would like to see us write that letter or make that phone call. Now I'm well aware that this sort of behavior will cause a considerable uproar. It will be a rattled bone that tries to make amends, and perhaps there will be much shaking and quaking, until we come together—but come together we must, if God is ever to bring renewal.

How can there be blessing if I am out of fellowship with a connecting bone? I remember being responsible for a youth work and suddenly becoming aware that my co-leader seemed distant. I realized that I must have offended her, but hadn't the remotest idea how or why. Now you would think it would have been the easiest thing in the world to simply ask her what I had done. But it wasn't the easiest thing in the world; it was the hardest. First of all, I didn't want to ask, because I really didn't want to hear the answer. I knew the verse that said, "Faithful are the wounds of a friend . . ." (Proverbs 27:6), but being very fond of myself, I didn't like wounds. *Why ask for trouble?* I thought. Surely it would be best to pretend I hadn't noticed that anything was wrong and hope it would put itself right. It seldom does, of course, and this particular situation simply deteriorated, until the atmosphere between us fairly crackled! In the end, I plucked up enough courage to ask her if something was wrong. We are such egotistical creatures that this is usually the way that we go about things. We won't say, "Have I hurt you?" or "What's wrong with me?" Instead we ask the other, "What's wrong with *you?*" In the end, my faithful friend told me that she had been offended by my bossy manner, and I was able to say how very sorry I was about it. It was not that my fellow worker resented my authority, but rather, my attitude. As the bones came together, we could work in harmony again.

There is nothing more painful than having a bone out of joint. Dislocated bones must be set in the proper relation to each other, if normal activity is to continue. As the bones come together and find their place in the body, the feeling of isolation is dealt with too. Bone needs bone. We cannot do without the other, and when we are truly connected, our gifts get detected, and we get elected to the right spot. The jawbone has to rest on the neck bone; the leg bone must lend its support to the foot bone, and then the whole body can begin to take shape and get moving.

But let's talk for a moment about the absolute necessity for prayer. Think about the bones in the valley. At this point we do not see bare bones—simply bored ones. There they lay, beautifully set in order at last—held together by sinews, fat with flesh and covered with skin, but still, only a crater full of corpses.

> When I beheld, lo, the sinews and the flesh came up upon them, and the skin covered them above: but there was no breath in them.

>   Verse 8

Everything had come together—but to what purpose? There was, as yet, no life in their frames, no spirit, or liveliness. And so Ezekiel prayed, for he knew it would have to be the Spirit that would quicken, so he prayed:

> . . . Oh, breath of God, come.

>   *See* verse 9

Oh, how we need to learn to pray as Ezekiel prayed. Do we know how to call for the breath of blessing? Many of us do not belong to boneyards full of bones, but to craters full of corpses.

Maybe the Word has been preached faithfully in our churches, and perhaps the substance has been given, the flesh and the sinews have gone up, and skin covers the whole. We may even be correctly connected to each other—*but* there is no life. The army marches not, the drum beat beats not, the battle battles not. But just watch what happens when we learn to pray!

> So I prophesied as he commanded me, and the breath came into them, and they lived, and stood up upon their feet, an exceeding great army.

> Verse 10

As Ezekiel prayed, the wind came, and the army stood up on their feet. Discovering that they had a backbone, instead of a wishbone, they were ready for the divine invasion.

> "If God be for us, who can be against us" they cried!
> Who indeed!
> But oh, if God be against us—who can be for us?
> Who indeed!

And, according to the Bible, we know that God is against dry, dusty, depressed, disintegrating disciples. He would not have us so, for He came to tell us personally that His wish is for us to have "life and to have it more abundantly" (John 10:10). He would bend the brittle bone with the breath of His blessing; He would bring renewal to us all!

> Breathe on me, Breath of God,
> Fill me with life anew,
> That I may love what Thou dost love,
> And do what Thou wouldst do.

> Breathe on me, Breath of God,
> Until my heart is pure,
> Until with Thee I will one will
> To do and to endure.

Breathe on me, Breath of God,
Till I am wholly thine,
Until this earthly part of me
Glows with Thy fire divine.

Breathe on me, Breath of God,
So shall I never die,
But live with Thee the perfect life
Of thine eternity.
                Amen.

EDWIN HATCH

WORKSHEET

Brittle Bones

Suggested time—10 minutes

1. The Bare Bones
    a) As a "born-again bone," have you ever been dry, depressed, or desolate? Why?
    Write a sentence about confusing numbers with blessings. Write another sentence about confusing busy-ness with blessing.
    b) Discuss the terms "divinity's diet" and "spiritual anorexia."

Suggested time—20 minutes

2. The Blessing Bone
    a) What does it mean to be "captured" [apprehended] by the Lord? (Read about Paul's experience in Philippians 3:12, 13.)
    b) Share an experience of being "carried" into a "dry" situation and what happened: to you; to the situation.
    c) Discuss the commands that Ezekiel was given in Ezekiel 37:4, 5, 6, 9.
    What did the Lord do for Ezekiel?
    What did Ezekiel do for the Lord (verses 7, 10)?

Suggested time—10 minutes

3. The Bound Bones
    Make a list of the things that have to happen before the bones can come together in the right place in the body. (Refer to 1 Corinthians 12:12–31.)

Suggested time—10 minutes

4. The Breathing Bones
    Without "The Breath of Blessing" we are in danger of being simply a crater full of corpses. We can have sinews, substance, and skin, but no Spirit that raises us up—up on our feet—and causes

us to be "ready to go." In the end all are dependent on Deity to deliver us from dead doctrine and use truth to set us free.

Suggested time—10 minutes

5. Prayer Time
   Spend time praying for the Breath of Blessing in:
   a) your own life
   b) the life of your church
   c) the nation
   d) the world

6

Gripy Grapes

Now will I sing to my wellbeloved a song of my beloved touching his vineyard. My wellbeloved hath a vineyard in a very fruitful hill:

And he [dug] it, and gathered out the stones thereof, and planted it with the choicest vine, and built a tower in the midst of it, and also made a winepress therein: and he looked that it should bring forth grapes, and it brought forth wild grapes.

And now, O inhabitants of Jerusalem, and men of Judah, judge, I pray you, [between] me and my vineyard.

What could have been done more to my vineyard, that I have not done in it? [Why], when I looked that it should bring forth grapes, brought it forth wild grapes?

And now . . . I will tell you what I will do to my vineyard: I will take away the hedge thereof, and it shall be eaten up; and break down the wall thereof, and it shall be [trampled] down:

And I will lay it waste: it shall not be pruned, nor digged, but there shall come up briers and thorns: I will also command the clouds that they rain no rain upon it.

For the vineyard of the Lord of hosts is the house of Israel, and the men of Judah his pleasant plant: and he looked for [justice], but behold oppression; for righteousness, but behold a cry.

Isaiah 5:1–7

*H*ow *to cope with trampling times, pressing pressures, and sour grapes.*

Vineyards were as much a part of biblical life as the hamburger to the American, a cup of tea to the British, or a sausage to the Pole! It is not surprising, therefore, to discover the figure of the vine scattered throughout the biblical record. Right at the beginning of the Book of Genesis, we read about Noah planting a vineyard.

Throughout Jeremiah and Ezekiel's writings there are numerous illustrations and applications concerning the vine, and in the New Testament, our Lord makes personal use of the figure—reminding us that unproductive vines are "good for nothing" (*see* John 15:5). The symbol of the golden vine adorned the gate of Israel's temple, and there is little doubt that the people associated it with the idea of fruitfulness and blessing.

The psalmist sang a happy song about a wife who was like "a fruitful vine by the sides of thine house: thy children like olive plants round about thy table" (Psalms 128:3). This did not mean that the man's wife was climbing the walls! The whole idea was that lots of children meant lots of work, and lots of work meant lots of cash, and lots of cash meant lots of prosperity.

In the spiritual as well as the natural sphere, the vine was associated with the potentiality essential to life. Israel knew that God intended them to be a grand demonstration of the fact that they belonged to Him, and therefore blessing was inevitable.

Thou hast brought a vine out of Egypt: thou hast cast out the heathen, and planted it.

Psalms 80:8

Joseph was described as ". . . a fruitful bough by a well; whose
branches run over the wall" (Genesis 49:22). In my horticultural ignorance, I have always imagined that vines needed to be supported
by a stake, like my tomatoes, but I learned from Scripture that pros-
perous vines crawl along the ground and grow over small walls,
comprised of the stones that litter the earth.

As Israel prospered beyond Joseph's day, Jehovah had been able
to say, "I had planted thee a noble vine, wholly a right seed . . ."
(Jeremiah 2:21). He had already promised that in Abram's seed ". . .
all the families of the earth [would] be blessed" (Genesis 12:3), for
He had worldwide celebration in mind. His Christ was to be the ultimate fruit of the vine of Israel. By the time we come to the major
prophets, however, God's choice vine was wildly out of control, and
Jehovah was heard to cry: ". . . how then art thou turned into the
degenerate plant of a strange vine unto me?" (Jeremiah 2:21).
Isaiah, aware that the figure of the vine would be well understood
by his contemporaries, used it in a parable to make his point.

And so let us listen to Isaiah's sad song and try to draw some
parallels for ourselves, because God intends for you and me, as He
did for Israel, a life of fruitfulness. It is often at *this* very point that
Christians experience their greatest failure. People do not see Christ
in us, and His risen life is not reproduced through our branches.
Sadly, many of us are no more like Jesus than the man in the moon,
even though we have known Him from our earliest days. Isaiah was
sent by God to warn Israel and all His people everywhere about this
very problem, and issue a call to repentance. First and foremost the
prophet's message concerned the *owner* of the vineyard. "Now will I
sing to my wellbeloved a song of my beloved touching his vineyard.
My wellbeloved hath a vineyard in a very fruitful hill" (Isaiah 5:1).

Jehovah was the vineyard's undisputed owner. The land was His
alone, for it had been created by His hand, and this theme is reiter-
ated late in the prophecy. "But now thus saith the Lord that created

thee, O Jacob, and he who formed thee, O Israel, Fear not: for I have redeemed thee, I have called thee by thy name; thou art mine" (Isaiah 43:1). Israel, created and redeemed, is seen to be the Lord's. No less are you and I. He created us and He redeemed us, and we belong to *Him*. Not only are we "once His" we are "twice His"! (I heard about a small boy who made a toy yacht. Finding a river, he sailed his craft along its winding streams, but the current being stronger than he supposed, carried the little ship away. Some time later, he looked into a shop window and saw his lost boat there. It had been found by the owner of the store and put up for sale. Hurrying inside, the small boy explained the situation, but the man was skeptical and demanded the child buy the toy. Nothing the little boy could say would change the man's mind, so in the end there was nothing to do but to pay for it. Hugging his boat to him as he left the shop, he said to it, *"Twice mine.* I made you, and now I've bought you—you're *twice mine!"*)

God made us, sailed us down the stream of life, and lost us to sin. He paid a great redemption price to buy us back—the life of His Son. Therefore He rightfully owns us. He is the undisputed possessor of our lives. We are twice His! Once we fully grasp that fact, we are well on the way to realizing some of the things that will begin to make us fruitful followers.

For example, if He is the owner of the vineyard of my life, then anything He allows to happen in *His* vineyard is *His* affair—not mine. All I have to do is to learn how to mind my own business. Gladys Aylward, a British missionary, living in wartime China, tells about the enemies' advance toward the town in which she lived. She decided to try to take the children in her care over the high mountains to freedom. Requested by a desperate father to take yet one more child, she refused and complained to God that it was not fair of Him to expect her to carry such a load. "I can't care for them all, Lord," she cried. Graphically relating Jehovah's reply, she told us that "God leaned out of heaven and retorted, 'Gladys Aylward, mind your own business'!"

I can remember a time when I talked to God as Gladys Aylward had talked to Him. It was during the period when my husband was involved in an itinerant preaching ministry and was hardly ever around. Loneliness caused me to forget that if God owned me then, that included all that I owned, even my husband. Jehovah leaned out of heaven and told me to mind *my* own business, too! He did it as He has done it so often, by leaning out of His Word. I was reading a parable in the Gospels about the owner of a vineyard who was hiring workers. A few were complaining about the length of time some servants worked, while others stood around idle, half the day. They didn't like the conditions, and they didn't like the pay (Matthew 20:1–16). It struck me that this was exactly the reason I was so angry. Why didn't He put the Christians who were hanging around doing next to nothing to work, so that my husband could stay home for a change? But now the Lord of the vineyard was asking me, "Is it not lawful for me to do what I will with mine own? . . ." (verse 15). Inasmuch as I acknowledged His ownership, there was *no* arguing with that.

If God owns our vineyards, then it follows that whatever He wishes to do with them and in them is His business, not ours.

This may sound a little rough, but I believe it is softened by the next fact that we learn from the passage. We discover that God is not just the owner of the vineyard, but that He is the lover of the vineyard, too.

"Now will I sing to my *wellbeloved* a song of my *beloved* touching his vineyard. My *wellbeloved* hath a vineyard in a very fruitful hill" (Isaiah 5:1, *italics mine)*. This is truly a love song! Isaiah loves Jehovah, and Jehovah loves him, and he knows it. What is so important is that he goes on knowing it, even when some pretty rough things begin to happen. The tough time is the very time that we need to remind ourselves that what He has allowed, He has allowed in love!

Isaiah was personally convinced of God's love at all times. Such sure knowledge helped him to react rightly to what God was doing in his own life, and in the life of his nation. Every time a judgment came Israel's way, Isaiah stubbornly refused to doubt the love of God. He determined to "mention the lovingkindnesses of the Lord, and the praises of the Lord, according to all that the Lord hath be-

stowed on us, and the great goodness toward the house of Israel,
which he hath bestowed on them according to his mercies, and according to the multitude of his lovingkindnesses" (Isaiah 63:7).

As Israel rebelled and the judgment of God fell, Isaiah set it all
against the background of the love of God, and sense was made of
toil and terror in his mind.

We must try not to meet the storms of life with the question
"How could He allow this terrible thing to happen if He loves us?"
Instead, we need to put our trust in His love, and then we will find
an anchor for our heart, and peace of mind in the midst of our adverse circumstances.

We knew a man in England who had no child. He and his wife
had prayed long and hard that God would grant them a little one to
brighten their days. The man lived in a depressed area of Britain
and worked in a huge industrial plant. The work at the plant was
greatly influenced by a Communist-dominated union, and most of
the man's fellow workers were of that particular political persua-
sion. Because the man was a Christian, he didn't have an easy time
of it. Then one day his wife told him that she was pregnant! Their
joy knew no bounds, and somehow the man's work in this hostile
environment took on a whole new perspective. It was easier now to
bear the snide remarks, or even the silent treatment meted out as a
favorite way of punishing a worker who wouldn't conform to the
popular pattern.

The time came for their baby to be born, and you can imagine the
shock, when the baby girl was born mongoloid. Now the couple had
to face the fact that their long-awaited child was not perfect and
would require a life of service and sacrifice on both of their parts.
But this was not the only sorrow they had to grapple with. The wife
knew she needed to tell unbelieving relatives, and the man thought
of the people he would have to face at work. How could he go back
and tell his workmates what had happened? What would they say?
But even that unpleasant thought paled into insignificance beside
the nagging doubts that wouldn't go away concerning the heart of
his God. *Were he and his wife truly loved?* How could a God who

loved them truly allow such tragedy to come into their lives? With much still unresolved in his mind, he returned to work. His fears had been justified, as the men gathered around to cruelly tease and terribly taunt him.

"How is it, you serve God, and He gave you 'half a child,' " they asked him gleefully. "And how is it, we don't even believe God exists, and our children are healthy and beautiful!" Standing there in the midst of that arena of arrogant atheism the man bowed his head. Shame filled his heart, for he knew that those voices were but an echo of his own doubts. But for that hour he had been given the Holy Spirit, whose work it was to assure him he was truly loved whatever happened to him.

Suddenly the man looked up, and his tormentors were amazed at the change in his face. He smiled and was content. A hush fell, as quietly the man said, "I'm so glad, *so* very glad, my God gave her to me and not to you!" In his great personal trouble, he refused to doubt the love of God and determined in the face of apparent disaster to "mention the lovingkindnesses of the Lord, and the praises of the Lord, according to all that the Lord hath bestowed on [him] . . ." (Isaiah 63:7).

In response to his faith, the man found an anchor for his heart and a peace of mind that passed all understanding—for he discovered that not only was God the Owner of his vineyard and the Lover of his soul, He was the husbandman, too.

Now a husbandman is a farmer. God is not the sort of owner that buys up a vineyard and then proceeds to abandon it, or hire it out to strangers. He comes Himself to farm it. He gets His hands involved in our affairs.

In ancient times, a tower was built in the midst of the vineyard to serve various functions. At harvesttime, it provided accommodation for the family who owned the property. They would move into the room at the base of the tower, and stay there until the whole process was finished. What an incredibly tender picture this gives us. We can know the reality of the presence of the Family at harvest time! The Holy Trinity will abide in the room of our soul, so that we can count on the presence of the Father, the succor of the Son, and the enabling of the Holy Spirit. They will whisper love to our hearts in the midst of all of our trials. But many a Christian complains bitterly that it is not enough to have the Godhead whisper "lovingly" in their ears, and it seems impossible to produce Christlikeness in their sad situations. In fact, they will tell you they are having a terrible job simply surviving. The Owner, Lover, and Farmer of our souls, however, has been about His business so thoroughly, He has prepared the soil of our hearts for a potential harvest. For example, He has planted His vineyard with *the choicest vine*. Now we all know who *that* is, don't we? Our Lord Jesus Christ Himself called Himself "the vine" (John 15:1).

God has planted us with Christ. When you said the prayer, when you invited Jesus into your heart, when you committed your life to Him, when you asked the Holy Spirit to invade your personality, then God responded and planted you with His Choicest Vine. The very life of Christ was rooted in your soul, and no man can pluck Him out. No enemy, no friend, not even your very own hands, can tear His eternal life from your heart. He is planted there forever.

Suppose someone close to you dies. How are you going to show serenity and victory over death, if you haven't faced it yourself? How will you overcome the grief that overcomes you? Well, He has both faced it and overcome it, and for *this* you have Jesus, because you have been planted with Him.

But farming the vineyard involves an awful lot more than merely planting it. Farming involves *farming*. It means digging out the stones and preparing the ground. I get the idea from this parable that the owner of the vineyard was determined to leave no stone unturned in the preparation of the land. He wanted to give the vine as much opportunity as possible to spread and to grow. It was therefore of utmost importance to clear the ground. If the holy life of the Owner is to be evident at all, there will certainly have to be a gathering out of the stones that litter our thoughts and our deeds. There will need to be a digging into our past and a turning over of our present. There will be sorrys that need to be said, and reconciliations made, and anything that stops the spreading vine will have to be dealt with. There is little fruit produced from stony ground, but God will help us! He will get down in all the muck and mire and farm us, helping to rid the soil of all the blockages, so that it can breathe again. There is absolutely no limit to the involvement of Jehovah in our lives. He has given Himself exclusively to us, and for this reason, expects to see fruit produced so that we and the world around us may celebrate together, and that He may be glorified.

With all this in mind, is it any wonder that the Owner of the vineyard asks the rhetorical question: "What could have been done more to my vineyard, that I have not done in it? [Why], when I looked for it to bring forth grapes, brought it forth wild grapes?" (Isaiah 5:4). The vineyard's location was quite excellent, having been established in a "very fruitful hill." There had been enough warm sunshine to ensure sweet grapes, and there had been excellent exposure to catch the gently falling rain. Carefully and lovingly, the choicest vine had been planted, and the whole project had had the wholehearted involvement of the whole Family. A lookout had even been posted at the top of the tower—to make sure no enemy came to spoil the crop.

It is in the Song of Songs we read about the little foxes that got among the vines and spoiled the fruit. The lookout watched for those small wastrels and warned of their approach.

There has been many a time that my Heavenly Lookout has alerted me to the approach of an enemy. Whether it has been a friend who tempted me to deny my faith, or my own intrinsic self-ishness that dared me do another down, or even Satan's subtle and snide suggestions along the way—I have been duly alerted to those little foxes!

I remember the time I was asked to speak at a big meeting. Finding a conflict of opportunity on that particular date, I wondered which of the two invitations to accept. On the one hand, a group of college kids needed encouragement, but on the other hand, a great chance had come my way to speak to thousands of women. What was I to do? At first, as I thought and prayed about it, I was honestly confused and the little foxes saw their chance! I was tempted to think of the numbers that were involved, and thought it would surely be a better stewardship of my time to accept the larger meeting. While I was debating the question, the phone rang. It was the organizer of the "big" opportunity who was calling to say she had omitted to tell me about the very generous honorarium they would like to give me, if only I would come. Now the little foxes really got among the vines! The Watcher in the tower directed my attention to the danger by a word from His Word: "Help me to prefer obedience to making money!" (Psalms 119:36 TLB). He couldn't have been much more explicit than that, and it then became a clear-cut choice of the mighty dollar or the Mighty Deity! In other words, it had become a question of what *He* wanted me to do.

Once I was willing to obey, it was not hard to know the right course of action to take. God had provided everything necessary for Israel to produce an abundant harvest, and when He asked the question, "What could have been done more to my vineyard than I have done in it?" the answer was very obvious to Isaiah: "Absolutely nothing!" And when He asks us the very same question, the answer is equally obvious. We live in a country of liberty, surrounded by plenty, and lack for nothing to keep us healthy, wealthy, and wise. We have full access to the sunshine of Christian fellowship, and the soft rainfall of prayer. We have been given a Watchman in the tower of our spirit, and have been planted with His choicest vine, so that when He asks, "Why the gripy grapes?" we must respond softly, *"Why indeed?"* So then, how can my life, pressed by my problems, result in the wine of celebration?

If I can only understand that a vineyard without harvesttime is like a doughnut without a hole, then I might begin to produce some fruit. Can you imagine a vineyard piled two miles high with grapes that haven't been pressed? That would be ridiculous, yet often I hear Christians complaining about the pressures and troubles that come their way, as if they expected their lives to be piled two miles high with God's blessings and kept that way. If only we could begin to expect harvesttime! Isaiah tells us that there is a winepress in the vineyard, and it follows that there has to be pressing out of the life of the Vine, if the world is to know what it is to celebrate.

In ancient days, grapes were pressed in different ways. The trampling method is the one that is perhaps the most familiar. On a certain day, when the fruit was judged to be ripe, everyone had a great time "treading the vine"! We've all seen pictures of that event, and noted what a jolly time was had by all; all, that is, except the poor old grapes. This gives us a good illustration of one way God uses to press us out. Sometimes people are allowed to climb into our relationships and trample all over our feelings.

"Are you telling me that I need to allow people to walk all over me?" you ask. No, I'm certainly not. I don't believe we should allow people to walk all over us, but sometimes there is absolutely nothing we can do to stop them. I remember being a very new and inexperienced pastor's wife, and enduring a traumatic trampling time. Funnily enough it was not *I* who was being trampled, but rather my husband. It was his reputation and motives that were being questioned. At first I produced some pretty sour grapes about the criticism, but the Holy Spirit helped me to recognize the fact that harvesttime had arrived. Then I remembered the Family was in residence and for *this I had Jesus!* I knew I had been planted, farmed, and readied for this very moment. It was now up to me to let Him produce sweet wine under those trampling feet. His patience and His self-control needed to be manifest, instead of my sour remarks; His forgiving Spirit needed to flow forth instead of my retaliating one. The end result—*celebration!* Joy will always be the case, when things are working rightly in the vineyard.

The grapes were also pressed another way. In Bible times, the people set a big stone in a trough and moved it slowly over the grapes, with monotonous regularity. It is not always the big troubles—the many trampling feet or the huge crushing crisis that does the trick—but, rather, the mundane pressures of day-to-day living. I'm speaking of ongoing pressures that never seem to go away—like having to live with someone who is quite impossible to live with. I remember the time a difficult relative came to live with us. This particular lady pretty well disapproved of everything that went on in our home, and I discovered that it is a very heavy thing to live with disapproval. However, once I realized what was happening, God helped me to work it out. I came to see that the Lord was looking for the fruit of acceptance and sweet understanding on my part. It took that particular circumstance to give Him the opportunity to crush it out of me.

Grapes are also pressed *by each other!* When you get a good healthy bunch of grapes that are growing in close proximity, they tend to bring such pressure to bear on one another, they force a flow of wine. This is surely one of God's favorite ways of harvesting His vineyard. The Bible teaches us that those of us who are believers should belong to a bunch. Maybe you have joined a bunch of Bible-believing Presbyterians, perhaps Baptists, or maybe Pentecostals, and, yes, Methodists! It doesn't really matter what the bunch is called, as long as you are part of one. After all, there is nothing so sad as seeing one grape left sitting all alone on a bunch. If the bunch is healthy, there will be plenty of pressing situations going on. You will find, for instance, that God invariably seems to place you next to the very grape you simply cannot abide. Well, He has done so for a good reason—celebration! Try to realize that it is harvesttime, and allow that realization to affect your relationship and to bring forth whatever aspect of the fruit of the Spirit that is needful in your character.

A long time ago, while in hospital, I met a girl whom I disliked at first sight, and the feeling was obviously mutual. After both of us were discharged, she joined my church, which really bothered me, until I realized we belonged to such a large fellowship, that we would never need to meet. I could go to *this* meeting, and she could go to *that* one. Then, one day as I signed up for a convention, I saw her name on the list. *Never mind,* I thought, *I'll put my name at the bottom as hers is at the top!* I was careful to note which bus she boarded and chose another. Arriving at the small town where the meetings were to be held, I was slightly flustered to discover we were assigned to the same hotel. Making a quick reconnaissance of the facilities, I was relieved to find two dining halls. Good! We could eat in different locations. Climbing the stairs to my bedroom, I met *her* at the door. *Oh, surely not?* I cried silently. Surely so. We were to share. My dismay turned to horror, as we entered our quarters and discovered—one bed. God has a weird sense of humor. It was harvesttime for us. He forced us both to get to know the other, and soon brought joy out of our pressured situation. When He chooses to place you together in His bunch with—*whomever*—sit still. Let it happen—He knows what He is doing.

In the end, producing fruit demands cooperation from us, for we have the dreadful privilege of deciding to be or not to be pressed out in celebration. We can so easily lose sight of God's eternal purposes, and refuse to cooperate with the Owner, Lover, and Farmer of our souls. If we do so, the warning of Scripture is somber and clear.

> And now . . . I will tell you what I will do to my vineyard: I will take away the hedge thereof, and it shall be eaten up; and break down the wall thereof, and it shall be [trampled] down: And I will lay it waste: it shall not be pruned, nor digged; but there shall come up briers and thorns: I will also command the clouds that they rain no rain upon it.
>
> Isaiah 5:5, 6

Not for me—the broken wall, the humbled hedge, the hardened soil. God forbid that He should command His clouds to rain no rain upon me.

Jehovah warns us that "He shall lay the vineyard waste." Wasted and not watered? Briers instead of blessing? No way! For me the trampling of my life by my Lord's displeasure is a far greater tragedy to be feared than the trampling of mere human feet.

We need to remember that the Owner, Lover, and Farmer of our vineyard is also in the last resort to be our *Judge,* as well.

> Deepen all Thy work, O Master,
>   Strengthen every downward root;
> Only do Thou ripen faster,
>   More and more Thy pleasant fruit;
> Purge me, prune me, self abase;
>   Only let me grow in grace.

Let me grow by sun and shower,
  Every moment water me;
Make me really, hour by hour,
  More and more conformed to Thee,
That Thy loving eye may trace
  Day by day my growth in grace.

F. R. HAVERGAL

WORKSHEET

Gripy Grapes

Suggested time—6 minutes

1. Read Isaiah 5:1–7. Then review the following verses:
   Psalms 128:3   Psalms 80:8   Genesis 49:22
   Jeremiah 2:21   Genesis 12:3
   Discuss the figure of the vine in Israel's thinking.

Suggested time—6 minutes

2. Jehovah is revealed as the Owner, Lover, and Farmer of the vineyard. Which "picture" means the most to you, and why? (*A few sentences from each participant.*)

Suggested time—15 minutes

3. The Lord Jesus Christ said, "I am the vine, ye are the branches." Read John 15:1–8.
   The believer's vineyard has been planted with God's choicest vine—Christ Himself.
   a) What, then, are the conditions of fruitfulness?
   b) What do you think pruning means?
   c) What warnings are here?
   d) What can we do without Him?
   e) Which verse do you like the best? Why?
   f) Which verse do you like the least? Why?

Suggested time—10 minutes

4. Share, if appropriate, some of the little foxes that have spoiled the fruit in your life. (*A few sentences will do!*)
   Review the three ways of pressing grapes:
   a) the trampling
   b) the continuous pressure
   c) the bunch
   Which of these illustrations can you identify with and why?

Suggested time—10 minutes

5. Suggested *Memory Verse:* Isaiah 5:4
"What could have been done more to my vineyard, that I have not done in it? [Why], when I looked that it should bring forth grapes, brought it forth wild grapes?"

Suggested time—10 minutes

6. Prayer Time
Read Isaiah 5:5, 6 and the last paragraph of this chapter to the group.
Pray about it. If you do not wish to participate by praying out loud, simply say, "Pass," when your turn comes.

7
Burdened Brothers

Come unto me, all ye that labour and are heavy laden, and I will give you rest.

Take my yoke upon you, and learn of me; for I am meek and lowly in heart: and ye shall find rest unto your souls.

For my yoke is easy, and my burden is light.

Matthew 11:28–30

To *"bear a bearable burden" is an art in itself; a skill the Lord Jesus wishes us to acquire; and a problem He addressed while here on earth.*

One day Jesus issued a gracious invitation to all "who labored and were heavy laden to come to Him and He would give them rest." The Greek word that is translated "labour" is κοπιάω and is used in the sense of toiling to the point of acute weariness. Paul talks about this and tells us, "We ought to labor, to support the weak, because it is more blessed to give than to receive" (*see* Acts 20:35). The weak he referred to in this case were the materially poor. Paul, though a missionary, took care of his own expenses by tentmaking and also earned enough on the side to look after his traveling companions' needs. On top of all that, he was able to give generously to the needy he met along the way. "You know," he told the Ephesian elders, "that these hands of mine worked to pay my own way . . ." (Acts 20:34 TLB); and to the believers in Corinth he wrote, "To this very hour we have gone hungry and thirsty, without even clothes to keep us warm. We have been kicked around without homes of our own. We have worked wearily with our own hands to earn a living . . ." (1 Corinthians 4:11, 12 TLB). Paul knew what it was like to labor and in the laboring, grow weary. In fact the apostle was able to say, "I Paul labor more than all—warning every man and teaching every man in all wisdom that we may present every man perfect in Christ. For this I 'labor' striving according to his work which worketh in me mightily!" (*See* Colossians 1:28, 29.) Not

129

only was Paul doing his bit supporting society, and supporting himself, he was doing more than his share by supporting the saints as well. You can grow pretty tired with all of that.

So if you were wondering if the Lord Jesus meant *you* when He said "Come unto *Me*"—ask yourself the question: "Am I tired to the point of exhaustion, trying to make ends meet—laboring with my own hands to put food on the table and clothes on my family's back? Am I working to support the weak and doing more than my share in my community? And am I growing weary supporting the saints, as Paul supported them?" (After all, it takes a certain sort of energy to warn *every* man and teach *every* man, so that we can present *every* man perfect in Christ!)

I think of the spiritual responsibility we have as believers in Jesus. Preaching reminds me of a man taking a bucket of water and throwing it over a crowd. The people are like bottles, and the preacher hopes against hope that, in the process, some of the bottles will catch some of the water. On the other hand, personal discipleship, which is working one by one with people, can be likened to someone's taking the same bucket of water, and carefully pouring the contents into each and every bottle, making sure they are filled to the brim. Now *that* is a wearisome business. It is also a necessary business and is not just for the so-called professional Christian, but for everyone of us who loves the Lord.

Someone has said it takes 5 percent effort to win someone to faith in Christ but 95 percent toil and trouble to help them to grow to maturity. I'm sure that that is true. Once you help someone into the Kingdom of God, you are under an obligation to support him as he explores it. Imagine a midwife assisting in the birth of a baby— and then abandoning it the minute it is born! Paul talked in the strongest possible terms about the labor it would take to bring young believers to maturity. It was a constant burden to him, a burden he did not shirk but a burden nevertheless. Maybe God will use you to help a young teenager accept Christ. You will find you have a spiritual baby on your hands—one who is most demanding. She will be hungry and need to be taught how to feed on the "sincere milk of the Word" for herself. She will have to be protected from disease and danger, and that could mean getting up very early in the morning before you go to work to engage in a spiritual battle of prayer on her behalf. She will need exercise, as she begins to stretch and grow, and that will lead to finding ways of helping her to witness—even if that involves her bringing groups of friends by to meet you, so that you can deal with their questions. It may be they will eat your cookies, and trample all over your carpets in their wet shoes, and keep you up well past your bedtime, disturbing your jealously guarded routine.

It could even be that you will stumble into trouble, ending up at the police station in the middle of the night, trying to understand what went wrong with all your good intentions, and realizing you may have to begin all over again, building new bridges of trust or mending a broken heart. One thing will probably lead to another, and very soon you may meet Mom and Dad who are busy getting a divorce and have forgotten all about the children in the melee. They may reach out to you for counsel, hoping their marriage can be saved. You could even find yourself sitting between them at three o'clock in the morning, while they scream unmentionable insults at each other over your head!

As you wonder how on earth you got yourself into all of this, you may catch a glimpse of Grandma, sitting in unspeakable anguish in a rocking chair, cradling her agony, and crying out silently for mercy. *What will become of her if the parents separate,* you wonder?

They do separate, and suddenly you are using your savings to move Granny into a "home," but when you and Granny get there, it's so bad you know you can't possibly leave her. So you bring her back, wondering what your husband will think, when you ask him to remodel the basement to make it nice and cozy for Granny in wintertime. The problem is that you can't get that "home" and those haunted faces of the other grandmas and grandpas out of your dreams. Your dreams are turned into visions, as you plan outings and special services for them at Christmas. If you could only write a little drama and encourage some of the teenagers to sing some songs—but that will mean rehearsals and phoning and persuading someone to come and play the piano; or hiring a piano for the someone you hope to persuade to play—to *play!* Then, of course, you'll have to cancel your tennis appointment to stand in line and collect Granny's Social Security check. Then there will be the hours and hours spent fighting city hall, because they don't understand the situation now she's living in *your* basement! "Did you know," they will ask you, "that it's not all that healthy underground for an old lady; and, of course, you'll need to knock a hole in the living room floor to put in a fire exit." (This is called *ministry,* folks!)

You don't go out to become a minister in grand style. You start to care just where you are, and one thing will lead to another, until before you know it, you will be "full time" for God. All this can happen while you are trying to balance your responsibilities to your own family and home, as you raise your children, turn up at their PTA meetings, and plan that special missionary trip with your husband to find out firsthand how you can get more involved in your church's missions program. The events I have described are normal labors of love for those who are committed to the Lord Jesus Christ, but sometimes they can lead us to become so burdened we crack under the strain.

Have you ever seen the man in the circus, who starts a plate spinning, and then another, and then another? In the end, he has a dozen or so, revolving at the same time but at various speeds and in different places. His job is to keep the momentum going. The expert makes it look easy, tapping this one, skipping over to a wobbly disk to give it an extra whirl—and drawing admiring gasps of appreciation from the audience. I have often felt like that artist, except I'm not the expert, performing smoothly and easily in front of the crowd. I am the amateur, learning the trade, panicking, or dashing here and there, picking up the broken plates I couldn't stop from falling. I know what it is to finish up tired out from trying to keep every plate spinning. I understand a little of what Paul was talking about, when he said you can end up exhausted supporting yourself, supporting society, and supporting the saints.

The same Greek word that is rendered "labour" in our text can also be rendered "toil." In other Scriptures, too, where it is employed in the sense of a "striking beating trouble," it is used to describe the sort of situations that leave us with a chronic weariness. Jesus reminds us of some familiar questions that people were asking in His day, such as, "What shall we eat and what shall we wear, and how much money can we make?" Struggling to find answers to those problems can result in "striking beating trouble" that leaves us whipped and whimpering. People can worry themselves into weariness over such matters of everyday living from positions of wealth, as well as from positions of poverty. I know women in comfortable, wealthy suburbia who are chronically tired. Their condition no way reflects a lack of sleep. On the contrary, they have hours and hours of leisure and every night enjoy uninterrupted slumber in soft king-size beds. They are experiencing a weariness of another nature that can end up affecting them physically. It is a burdensome anxiety—a low-grade foreboding, that nags away all the time, persuading them to believe something is about to happen to spoil their way of life. This wears them out.

The word is used yet again in Luke's Gospel where the disciples tell of the frustration of *toiling* all night and catching nothing (Luke 5:5). It is very enervating to have all the right equipment; to have been trained by the experts for your job, and to do it in the right way—but to bring nothing home at the end of the day. When you have no fish in your nets (or, to change the analogy—no people in the pew), it's time to come to Christ and find out what's wrong. I know Christians who have been to the best of seminaries, listened to the best teachers, learned the best methods of evangelism, interned with the best masters, and having received their own pastorate, have toiled faithfully and diligently all night—and yet have caught nothing! Growing weary beyond measure, they have simply quit. Now that's a shame. Because it is to people like that the invitation of Jesus Christ has been given. "Come unto Me—*all* of you!" He says, "and I will give you rest!"

Anyone would grow weary with the loads I have tried to describe, if they were to bear them alone. There are, of course, many people who carry next to nothing through life. They are adept at finding others to shoulder their personal burdens for them, and they sail along, never feeling a need to borrow a shoulder! But many others carry a disproportionate weight, while some bear seemingly unbearable burdens.

The word *laden* is used to describe a boat that is about to sink. We find the picture framed for us in the story of Paul's shipwreck. The apostle, who was a prisoner at the time, was being transported to Rome by boat. Since he knew the Knowing One, he knew things others knew not, and perceived that the journey would not be without loss.

"Sirs," he cautioned the captain and centurion, "this voyage will be with injury and much damage, not only of the 'cargo' but also of our lives" (*see* Acts 27:10). The word that Paul used here describing the "cargo" or "lading" of the ship is our word *laden.* This picture gives us a graphic figure of a sinking saint. Perhaps today, as you read this book, you are feeling like a little boat—*laded* in every nook and cranny—straining in the hold.

"Come unto Me all who are growing weary to the point of exhaustion, and who have been loaded with burdens, and are bending beneath their weight," invites Jesus. What is the heavy weight that "lades" you down? Can you identify the burden you bear that is demanding all of your resources?

When I was a little girl, I lived in Liverpool. My city was and still is a port, harboring ships of every size and shape imaginable. My father took me down to the docks one day to watch the cargo ships being loaded. Seeing quite a small boat being readied for its voyage, I asked my father, "However they would get all the cargo in its little tiny hold?" He pointed out the waterline that circled the vessel, and explained that this would help the dockers to gauge the lading process. Too light a load would leave the waterline above the water and mean the ship was "unfulfilled," while too much cargo would take the waterline below the water and pose danger. Do you get the point? The little boat needed enough of a burden to full/fill it, and not too much to sink it. Since those days long ago, when I was a little girl clutching my daddy's hand as we watched the boats, I have seen myself in that vivid illustration, as I have become tied up by my Christian commitment to the dockside of God's service.

I think of all the people who have stood on the dock and have loaded my boat for me: my boss, my husband, my church, my friends, my children, and the young people I ministered to for twelve years—and *me*. Yes, I think of the times I, too, have loaded my own boat! For a long time I didn't know about that waterline. I didn't understand the secret of "bearing bearable burdens," and I know about that awful sinking feeling, as I overloaded and disappeared under the waves. There have been many times that all that there has been left of me has been a little flag of distress. I didn't know God had made me with a carefully designed carrying capacity, and that I needed to watch the waterline.

Are you identifying with all of this? Have you been laboring? Are you overloaded? Just where is your waterline at the moment? If you are laded to the point of no return, then it is high time you were lightened. Someone needs to unlade your boat for you. You need balancing up by the Bearer of bearable burdens Himself—Jesus Christ.

Let's think about this for a minute. What sort of cargo do we bear that can sink us? First of all, there is the cargo of sin. A guilty conscience is fatiguing. It's heavy. But then there is necessary guilt and unnecessary guilt. Necessary guilt tells us that we are guilty, that we have broken God's rules, and that He is angry with us. It makes us feel bad, so that we want to get rid of the weight of it. Jesus Christ died to unload that sense of guilt off our boat. When we ask Him to forgive us, He will lighten our ship. This necessary guilt should drive us to the bearer of such burdens. We cannot unload that particular burden ourselves. Only God can do that for us.

The writer of the Book of Lamentations laments that the burden of sin is like a yoke and that this "yoke of his transgressions has come upon his neck" (*see* Lamentations 1:14). If I come into a personal relationship with the One who "bore my griefs and carried my sorrows," He will lighten that load for me. So sin can be the cargo that is sinking me. Second, I can sink myself! I need to know my limitations. This is where we come back to the illustration of the waterline. Every vessel is different. The battleship can carry so much more than the sailboat; the cargo vessel more than the tugboat. We need to take a good, hard look at the design of our particular bark, and this will give us a realistic gauge of the weight we should carry. I have always tended to pass a boat in midocean that is carrying more than I am, and find myself determining to take on more cargo at the first opportunity. Here I am, a medium-sized cargo vessel, competing with an aircraft carrier. This is just plain silly, but I have done it anyway. My own self-expectations have weighted me down well beneath the water, and I have found myself plowing through the swell, taking an inordinate amount of time arriving at my destination because of it. When a boat is overloaded, it *never* makes good time!

It is very helpful to have a husband, a friend, a child, or a pastor who will help us to identify the structure of our boat. This way, we come to know our carrying capacity, so that we can keep balanced. I am blessed with a husband who constantly adjusts my cargo for me. When he sees me listing to starboard, he sits me down and asks me how come I'm in such cockeyed shape! Not long ago, I was very busy overloading my ship, trying to find space for a cargo of book contracts—*six* in all. Observing my little flag of distress waving feebly in his direction, and seeing I was about to disappear under the billows without trace, my husband drew alongside and told me to take an inventory of the cargo I had taken on board; he wanted to inspect it. He thoughtfully examined each item on my list, and then taking a pencil, he struck a line through three books and unloaded my ship. "Keep these three assignments on board," he said. "They will be a heavy load to carry, but I think you can and should bear them to their destination [the publishing house]. These three," he continued, referring to the unloaded loads, "are well worth carrying, but will have to wait for the next voyage. I know you well enough," he concluded, "to know you cannot carry any more cargo at the present time; after all, I need some shirts washed." The Lord Jesus Christ can use all sorts of inspectors to help us balance our load. In this instance, He used my husband.

Maybe the cargo that is sinking us is not the cargo of sin or of self, but is a matter of the very situation we find ourselves in. Job had this to say about his circumstances:

> . . . I am full of tossings to and fro unto the dawning of the day. . . .
> My days . . . spent without hope. . . . my soul chooseth strangling and
> death rather than my life. . . . I am a burden to myself.
>
> Job 7:4, 6, 15, 20

Can't you just see Job's little boat, wallowing in the waves, as it was battered by the storm? Job had a wife who was like a millstone around his neck, teenagers who were heavy on his mind, and a business that had sunk. He was bearing boils, carrying cares, and all in all felt his little craft was all but lost! Maybe some of Job's kind of cargo is causing us craft problems, too?

Perhaps it is a question of another sort of weight altogether—that of old age. The writer of the Book of Ecclesiastes said that in our latter days even "the grasshopper shall be a burden" (Ecclesiastes 12:5). Maybe you can't cope like you used to; or can't get everything accomplished you'd like to; you seem to need more sleep than there is time for, and even the sign of a little-bitty bug takes you down under. In other words, the burden of old age is sinking you.

Not long ago I had to get glasses. I suppose I have really done very well to get to my 40s without having to use them, but as I left the optician, I felt as if I must look at least 104. It was a most depressing day. Returning home, I was not amused to read a little poem a friend (?) had sent me:

> My glasses come in handy,
>   My hearing aid is fine,
> My false teeth are just dandy,
>   But I sure do miss my mind!

It may be old age or young age, your marriage or your singleness—good times or bad times—whatever it is, you need to identify the cargo you are carrying, and then hear Christ say to you, "Come unto Me."

"Well," you say, "how will He help if I do come to Him? And what do you mean 'come' anyway?" Well, you have to come near enough for Him to get His shoulder under the load. That means close enough for a yoke to be placed upon your neck, fastening you firmly in place at His side. A teenager once said to me, "Everyone keeps telling me to draw nigh to God, but I have a problem. How will I know when I'm *nigh?*" In other words, she was asking, "How nigh is nigh?" The answer to that is, that you will know when you are nigh, because the burden will be lifted when the yoke is in place. When you are fastened to Him, just like the animals of the East were fastened to each other, and you begin plowing the same furrow and pulling in the same direction, you will know you are *nigh*. He promises that this yoke will be "easy"—not in the sense of being no problem at all, but in the sense of being possible.

Jesus promised that His yoke would be easy and His burden would be light. The astounding thing about all of this is that the divine solution for our predicament is not to come to Him and have Him spirit away our burden, so we never see it again; but to have Him place *another one* upon us. "But I'm sinking already," we gasp. "How can God possibly ask me to carry anything else?" Well, you see, *if* the burden is the one He has asked us to bear, and *if* it is His yoke that He invites us to share, we will find that it will be a bearable burden. In other words, the burden He asks us to bear will not feel like a burden at all. It will feel like a blessing! It will be a restful sort of a thing. It's really a question of exchanging burdens. He tells us He will take the weight of the one that is sinking us and exchange it for one that won't.

"But how will I know if the thing that I have taken on is His idea or mine?" Well, we must see if we sink. That's one good way to find out. I am to learn from Him which load is to be *my* load and which is not. The burden He asks me to bear will even give rest to my soul. There is a definite release in taking on a job that God has had in mind for you from the foundation of the world. Sometimes people talk of church work as if it is their punishment! Folks have said to me, "I don't know how you can *bear* to travel so much; or have Stuart away from home all the time; or do so much in the church." My answer to those sorts of comments is always, "But it's not a punishment—it's a privilege; it's not a grief—but a joy; not a burden—but a blessing." That is because *He* has loaded me up, and therefore there is a strange restfulness, as I carry those responsibilities. It's as if I don't have the whole weight on me, which, of course, I don't!

The word *rest* means a release from weariness, not an absence of labor. It is not a rest of leisure or a brief season of relaxation, but rather a lasting state of peace and strength. The burden may not be removed, but Christ will enable us to be as happy with the burden as without it. It is the rest—not of a river locked in ice, but of a stream in repose.

In creation, the rest of God is exhibited as a sense of power which nothing wearies; this is the rest He offers to create in us. If we will come to Him and learn our lessons well, we will find our burdens can actually bring us joy. Our Teacher is meek and lowly of heart. If at first we fail to bear our bearable burden, He will be very gentle and kind to us. He will not yell at us or stand us in a corner.

"Well," you say, "one day we'll all get home to heaven and then it will be all over at last; there will be no more burdens to bear." *Wrong!* When you and I get to heaven, we will be given yet one more burden. "Well, then," I hear you say, "if that's the case, I'll be coming straight back!"

Listen! The Bible tells us that there is laid up for us one more piece of cargo that would be far too heavy for us to bear bearably down here. As the apostle Paul tells us, there will be an "exceeding and eternal weight of glory" waiting for us there (2 Corinthians 4:17).

In the story of Paul's shipwreck, we read in Acts that the boat crashed on the rocks, and the sailors, centurion, and the prisoners cast themselves into the sea. The Bible says that they all made it to shore on the wreckage.

I am quite sure some people's boats will steam into the port of heaven without so much as a scratch, and some will enter the heavenly portals with marks of great storms they have weathered. Some—like Paul's—will arrive reduced to a plank. But I'll tell you something—we'll all make it! And when we get there, what a welcome there will be. The heavenly vessel that our Eternal Shipbuilder has promised to provide for us there will be well able to carry the weight of glory that is to be our reward.

Two missionaries were returning home from a lifetime of foreign service. They traveled by boat and were delighted to find out that the president of the USA was actually a passenger. As they steamed into America, the bands were playing, the red carpet had been rolled out, and the streamers were fluttering in the breeze. Everyone was pleased to see the president. The missionaries thought the whole world must have turned out to welcome him. They had never seen so many people. After some of the excitement had died down, the old folk began to scan the faces on the quay side. Where was their family? And where was the representative of their mission board? And why wasn't a deacon from their supporting church waving up to them? They realized with a shock, there was nobody to welcome them home at all! Sitting down dejectedly on a seat, the couple held hands and asked God *why* it was when the president went abroad for a week's political mission, he returned to such a welcome, but when *they* had spent their entire lives in His service there was no one there to care? As they waited for God to answer them, they were aware that He was saying, "But you're not home yet!"

For those of you who are burdened brothers, I would encourage you to furrow patience. You're not home yet, but, oh, when you eventually arrive—how glad you will be that you bore the burdens that He asked you to bear.

> Cast thou thy care upon the Lord,
>   The care that loads thy heart;
> Take Him this moment at His word,
>   And let Him do His part.
>
> The need is deep, the care is great,
>   The burthen hard to bear;
> Roll it on Him with all its weight,
>   And leave it resting there.
>
> This heavy thing, it is His gift,
>   His portion, thee to bless;
> Give it Him back; what He shall
>   lift
>   No more on thee shall press.

Cast all thy care, and not a part
  The great things and the small;
The Lord's all-loving, mighty heart
  Has room and thought for all.

Yes, He will ponder every care,
  Consider each detail;
Thyself, thy burthen, let Him bear;
  He will not, cannot, fail.

H. MARY MOULE

WORKSHEET

Burdened Brothers

Suggested time—10 minutes

1. Discuss:
   a) Are you weary and heavy laden? Check the area of your heaviest responsibility.
      ————Supporting society
      ————Supporting yourself
      ————Supporting saints
   b) Where is your waterline at this present time? Why?

Suggested time—5 minutes

2. What are some of today's burdens that are sinking Christians?

Suggested time—10 minutes

3. (Work in twos)
   a) What sort of ship are you? Identify yourself:

cargo	battleship
submarine	fishing boat
skiff	food ship
gunboat (troubleshooter)	*Titanic*

   b) Tell your partner why you see yourself as such a ship.

Suggested time—6 minutes

4. Read Acts 27:14–20 and discuss:
   a) Who lightened Paul's ship?
   b) Who can I think of who could lighten mine?

Suggested time—6 minutes

5. In the light of this lesson, can you identify the burden He is asking you to bear?
   Write a prayer about it.

Suggested time—5 minutes

6. Prayer Time
   Pray the prayer you have written in your group.

8

Prodigal Prigs

And he said, A certain man had two sons:

And the younger of them said to his father, Father, give me the portion of goods that falleth to me. And he divided unto them his living.

And not many days after, the younger son gathered all together, and took his journey into a far country, and there wasted his substance with riotous living.

And when he had spent all, there arose a mighty famine in that land; and he began to be in want.

And he went and joined himself to a citizen of that country; and he sent him into his fields to feed swine.

And he would fain have filled his belly with the husks that the swine did eat: and no man gave unto him.

And when he came to himself, he said, How many hired servants of my father's have bread enough and to spare, and I perish with hunger!

I will arise and go to my father, and will say unto him, Father, I have sinned against heaven, and before thee,

And am no more worthy to be called thy son: make me as one of thy hired servants.

And he arose, and came to his father. But when he was yet a great way off, his father saw him, and had compassion, and ran, and fell on his neck, and kissed him.

And the son said unto him, Father, I have sinned against heaven, and in thy sight, and am no more worthy to be called thy son.

But the father said to his servants, Bring forth the best robe, and put it on him; and put a ring on his hand, and shoes on his feet:

And bring hither the fatted calf, and kill it; and let us eat, and be merry:

For this my son was dead, and is alive again; he was lost, and is found. And they began to be merry.

Now his elder son was in the field: and as he came and drew nigh to the house, he heard musick and dancing.

And he called one of the servants, and asked what these things meant.

And he said unto him, Thy brother is come; and thy father hath killed the fatted calf, because he hath received him safe and sound.

And he was angry, and would not go in: therefore came his father out, and intreated him.

And he answering said to his father, Lo, these many years do I serve thee, neither transgressed I at any time thy commandment: and yet thou never gavest me a kid, that I might make merry with my friends:

But as soon as this thy son was come, which hath devoured thy living with harlots, thou hast killed for him the fatted calf.

And he said unto him, Son, thou art ever with me, and all that I have is thine.

It was meet that we should make merry, and be glad: for this thy brother was dead, and is alive again; and was lost, and is found.

Luke 15:11–32

This story asks the question: "What is a nice Jewish boy like you doing in a pigsty?"

If there is one thing that the eleventh chapter of Luke teaches us, it is that God doesn't like losing things, but that He does love finding them! We understand the heart of God, when Jesus tells us that the Good Shepherd "has come to seek and to save that which is lost," and that He has other sheep that are not of His fold that He *must* bring. We sense the grief in the losing and the urgency in the searching and the joy in the finding. God is a *finding* God; Jesus is a *seeking* Saviour. When God lost touch with the man He had made in Eden, He cried out, "Adam, where art thou?" (*see* Genesis 3:9). The Lord Jesus Christ volunteered to come to earth to search him out. God doesn't like losing any valuable valuables. In Jesus' day things like sheep, coins, and sons were all of great value to their owners. If you had asked a shepherd the cost of a sheep, a woman how valuable a coin, and a father how precious a son, they would have told you there was nothing they wouldn't do to find such treasured possessions, should they lose them.

Jesus told a story about a father who lost *two* sons. Losing one son must have been bad enough, but to lose two had to be a huge tragedy. He didn't lose his boys to death; he lost them to life! He lost the opportunity to be their father, and they forfeited the chance to enjoy the many benefits and blessings of being his sons. Both were prodigals, and both have something to teach us.

First of all, they had a personal relationship with the father, for they had been born into his family. Their *relationship* depended upon their birth, but their *fellowship* upon their behavior. Stuart and I have two sons. If either one should kick over the traces, choosing to live a totally different life-style from the life we lead, our relationship would probably be strained, but nothing would change the fact that they would always be our sons, whatever pigsty they ended up in. The blood tie would still be there. Our life would still be in them, and so their relationship would always depend upon their birth, even though their fellowship would depend upon their behavior.

Have you ever wondered how it is possible to do everything as right as a Christian parent can—and end up with a prodigal son? I don't know the full answer to that puzzle, but I do have a few clues. I know enough godly parents who are praying about prodigal offspring to know that it is not at all an unusual occurrence.

The two boys in the story that Jesus told represent this predicament. These boys had a *blood* relationship with their father, because they had been *born* of him into a wealthy, privileged family. The inheritance they stood to gain was quite considerable. According to the custom of the day, the elder son would inherit two-thirds of his father's property and the younger son one-third of it. The law of Israel provided for the possibility of gifts being made over to the sons while the father was still living; and so when the boys came to ask for the portions of the land that belonged to them, we find the father complying with their request. "And he divided unto them his [inheritance]"(Luke 15:12).

I am quite sure that the Lord Jesus intended us to understand something of the character of God through the telling of this parable, and as we search these verses, we can indeed glimpse some tender touches of the Trinity! We notice, for example, that the father gave freely and liberally to his children, expecting nothing in return. In fact, we see other evidences of his generosity in the comment to the elder brother in verse 31, when he said, ". . . all that I have is thine." Not only did he give his older son his inheritance while he was alive, he was able to say that all he had left was available to him also. What givingness! The father's givingness is mirrored, too, in the prodigal's remark from the pigsty as he "came to

himself." Remembering his father's concern for his servants, he ru-
minated, "How many hired servants of my father's have bread
enough and to spare . . ." (verse 17).

We also see the love of God portrayed, as the father anxiously
watched for the return of his youngest son. The Bible says that he
saw him coming "while he was yet a great way off . . ." (verse 20).
He was found daily waiting and watching from the top of the flat
eastern roof of his house, hoping to catch a glimpse of the shape of
his beloved prodigal returning. Love waits long and love waits well
and love never gives up. It watches forever, straining its eyes for an
encouraging sign on the dusty horizon. Real love behaves like the
father in this story.

After many years, when the stumbling figure eventually did appear, we read that the father joyfully ran down the road to meet
him. Oriental people *never* run! It is not *done* to run! Just as in
England it isn't *done* to introduce yourself to a stranger. You have
to wait till someone else does that for you. Eastern manners prohibit
Orientals changing their pedantic pace, for such impulsive displays
of emotion are out of place. But Jesus wanted the world to know
that true agape love waits on tiptoe, ready to run toward the re-
pentant one.

In that patient patriarch, we see God's character displayed,
not only by his generosity and love, but also by his willingness to
forgive. See the tender touch—the kiss of welcome, and then the
restoring grace, symbolized by the robe, covering the rags of
wrongdoing. Notice the way the father asked the servants to bring
shoes for his boy's feet, to help him walk the way a son of his should
walk, and think about the ring placed upon his boy's finger, which
gave him the authority to execute his father's business. As our Lord
recounted this parable, Jesus was saying, in effect, this boy failed.
But he didn't fail to return in repentance to the father, and that's
when he began to succeed. He was also giving a powerful pattern
for parenting.

This boy could be likened to many born-again boys of believing
Christian parents. They belong to the Father, having received His
life and become recipients of all the benefits reserved for the sons of

the family. When we receive the Father's life through regeneration by the Spirit, Jesus becomes our brother, and we find ourselves "joint-heirs with Christ . . ." (Romans 8:17). It is not only possible to take all that for granted—but to take it all and run! There are spiritual riches that our loving and generous Heavenly Father has given us as our birthright in Christ, and on top of that, has told us that all that He has is ours! And yet many of us, and many of our children, still behave like prodigals.

Parents can be prodigals as well as sons. When I used to teach in Liverpool and wrestled with the bad behavior of street kids, my school principal commented that, in her opinion, we were dealing with delinquent parents, rather than delinquent children. Much of the time she was right. Perhaps we have not been like the loving, giving parent in this story. We may have neglected to teach our children about God, failed to be a good model, and have even wandered a long, long way from our own religious heritage. If so, it is little wonder that our kids take off for the pigsty. But then how can we hope to be perfect parents when we are such imperfect people? Well, if we are realistic, we must know we will never do it *all* right, but then we need never do it *all wrong* either. Parents fail, and children fail, but there is a:

> . . . fountain filled with blood,
> Drawn from Immanuel's veins;
> And sinners plunged beneath that flood
> Lose all their guilty stains.

WILLIAM COWPER

When we came to Christ, we confessed our sin and God forgave us for Christ's sake, but we do not stop sinning because we became Christians. God has promised to "cleanse us from all unrighteousness" (1 John 1:9). That word *unrighteousness* means "doing it all wrong"! As parents, some of us need to confess the fact that we did the wrong thing in a particular situation. As a prodigal parent, we need to return to the Father, too, and have Him cover our parental neglect with His robe of forgiveness. Failure need not be final. Just as the son came to his senses, so a prodigal parent can come home to his children and be reconciled. In Christ, there is pardon for prodigals: fathers, mothers, sons, and daughters!

But what can we learn from the father who represents God in this story that may help those of us who are not prodigal parents, but who are dealing with prodigal children? First of all, the father let his boys go. When the youngest one said, "Give me, give me, give me," taking off to waste his life and inheritance in rebellious living, the father let him go. He didn't run after him and force him back into the house. He didn't lock him up in his room and guard the door to prevent his escape. His son had come of age. He was too big for that sort of treatment. He was his own person, an adult with a mind of his own, and the dignity of free choice—and so the father had to let him go. How hard that must have been, and how hard it is for us to do the same. But there is one thing you can be sure of—if this is your case—and you have had to watch a child head for the far country—God knows what that feels like and for that reason He understands and will comfort you. Sit still at His feet and open the Book of Genesis. Read how Adam, His son, lived in paradise—but still went wrong. Even before Adam was created, there were sons of God in heaven—angels who became prodigals, leaving behind their first estate, their heavenly inheritance, to become followers of Satan and sons of the night. And so you can know that God knows what a parent of a prodigal feels like.

I will never forget introducing two mothers who had both lost sons to heroin addiction. Clasping each other tightly, one said fervently to the other, "You know what it is like, don't you?" Clasp the hand of God, because He knows, too. The time to run will come. If a child is bent on riotous living, it will usually do no good to run after him immediately. Arguing and pleading will seldom change his mind, if his mind is already made up, though obviously everything possible should be done to prevent a child's running away from home. But if the child's face is set toward the far country, there is nothing too much you can do about it. I always remember turning around in the kitchen to find our youngest son, Pete, in my way. He had at last arrived at eyeball level. "Move, Pete, move!" I snapped, as he stood there mischievously. "Make me!" he retorted, knowing full well I couldn't do that anymore. I can remember that frightening sense of helplessness, as I realized he was too big to push around anymore. When a child is set on rebelling, you have to play the waiting game, watching till you see him turn around to take his first step back toward you. Wait until his face turns again in your direction, and then will be the time to *run.* You will need to go to meet him then, reaching out to match his tentative steps homeward.

Are you ready for that? The father didn't make his son crawl up to his feet! He didn't make it hard for him. He did not decide to make him pay for all those miserable years of watching and waiting he'd suffered through. He *ran* toward him! And as the father did, no less must we. We have to "race with grace" toward a penitent prodigal. The father dealt very differently with each of his boys' dilemmas. Children are not the same, just as snowflakes, flowers, or noses, are not the same. Do you ever look at your children (or someone else's children), and wonder how the same parents produced such staggeringly different diversity within the same family?

Our two boys are total opposites. For instance, Dave is scrupulously tidy. While he was living at home before he got married, he used to leave his dirty washing to be collected in neatly folded piles. The pins that were not in use on his bulletin board were kept in straight lines. Pete, on the other hand, left his dirty washing anywhere it happened to land, and I don't think he knows what the word *tidy* means to this day. David tried his very hardest to graduate from high school *magna cum laude,* while Pete, much to his surprise, graduated *laude how come?* Yes, our boys are opposites, and I venture a guess that your children are too. One of the mistakes we make in dealing with prodigals is to treat them all the same. Both the boys in Luke 15 were far away from their father. One had physically left home, but the other who stayed put was just as far away from his father as his brother. You can live in the same house and yet be strangers. The father had to reach out to his elder son as well as his youngest son, in order to bring him *in.* He thoroughly knew each child. Both had failed to be the sons he longed for them to be, but both had failed in different ways and needed to be approached differently. One of our children might rebel and decide he doesn't want to go to church, but that doesn't mean the other ones will. One may struggle with pride and one with the pigsty, but both need help and understanding. Let's see how the father set about coping with the problem.

The first situation was probably easier to handle than the second. Children who take off into the pigsty are usually quite straightforward individuals. You usually know just where you are with them, because they don't pretend to be something they are not. They don't bother sitting in church when they are far from God, pretending that everything is all right. Many an evangelical child has ended up in a pigsty, as he and she have searched for their own identities, or a faith of their own and not one that is simply an extension of their mother's or father's. The pigsty, of course, was about as far away as a Jewish boy could get from his roots and heritage. (I'm sure you know what good believing Jews think about pork, and to find the young man in the story keeping swine meant he had just about hit rock bottom.) I just love the part of this narrative that tells me he came to his senses, while he was sitting hungry and half-naked in the middle of that mess. He wasn't in church and he wasn't watching the 700 Club on TV; and he wasn't even attending a Billy Graham Crusade; he was in a pigsty! But God answered his father's prayers, and the lad came to his senses, even though he had sold himself to a citizen of the far country. He made a decision to arise and return to his father, and he made it all on his own, without "Just as I Am" playing softly and encouragingly on the organ, or spending time in a Christian rehab center.

Now let me say I am all for TV ministry, Billy Graham, and Christian counseling. That is not the point. The point is that we musn't shortchange what the Holy Spirit is doing when our children are physically in the far country, without any apparent Christian influence, or seemingly out of the hearing of any church bell. We tend to think that God can't bring our youngsters around without our help. The boy made his decision all on his own, and because he knew enough about the character of his father, he took the risk of returning home. So take heart, those of you who keep telling God how to bring your children back, and are getting frustrated because He won't do what He is told. He is right there in the pigsty with them. You can bank on it. Trust Him to bring your child to his senses, and He will do it in His way, and in His time. But watch, when the child eventually does come around, that you are prepared by prayer. When the time comes that you eventually face each other, try and let him have his say, even if you have saved up ten years of words for that moment. Listen to the prodigal son: "Father, I have sinned against heaven, and in thy sight, and am no more worthy to be called thy son" (verse 21). Notice the father let him confess his sin, and say that he was sorry, but he didn't let him go on to say, ". . . make me as one of thy hired servants" (verse 19). He wouldn't let him say that, because *once a son, always a son.*

However we have abused our privileged relationship of sonship, our Heavenly Father will never relegate us to the status of a hired servant. There will be full and free forgiveness, and reinstatement into a position in the family, because we never stopped belonging, we only stopped *behaving.* Children who return from the pigsty need to know they can come home. Do they know we love them because they are *ours,* not because they did or didn't act as we wanted them to act? Do they know enough about our character that will encourage them to return? There is no record of any angry, hurt recriminations on behalf of the father in the story the Lord Jesus told.

Remember the very human reaction of Mary and Joseph, when Jesus was lost in Jerusalem? What relief, when after seeking Him sorrowing, they found Him. But their relief spilled over in angry words: ". . . thy father and I have sought thee sorrowing," Mary burst out accusingly (Luke 2:48). *You hurt us,* she was saying. She and Joseph had been frightened and upset. In effect, they were punishing Him for that, and asking Him how He could have hurt them in that way? If your boy or girl comes home, can you keep quiet about yourself, do you think? You need to spend the time before that grand reunion, asking God to help you receive that child without reading the riot act.

After bringing a message from 1 Corinthians 13 at a women's conference, a mother came to talk to me. Her daughter had left home some time before, after an ugly and very painful scene. Now she wanted to return. After hearing me explain that true love kept "no record of wrongs," she came to tell me that she hoped she could meet her daughter with a different attitude. "I was ready to hear her tell me that she had sinned," she said, "and I was all set to make sure she didn't forget any of the details!" That mother had carefully kept a mental record of her daughter's wrongs. But love doesn't do that. Real love discounts the hurt done to it and rejoices when truth wins out.

After the father had received the boy, he gave him something to do. The ring contained a seal that gave the wearer the authority to conduct another's business. How wise of the parent to know that the son would need to be shown he had truly been forgiven by being given some responsibility to fulfill. What better proof than a chance to represent his father? If we tell our children that "failure is never final," our words will be empty, unless we show them that we truly mean it by trusting them with some responsibility. This will give them the chance they are looking for to show us their repentance is real.

So often, if a child has let us down badly when we have trusted, it is very difficult to trust again. But a good parent trusts a second time—and even three or four times. After all, that is how our Heavenly Father deals with us when we let Him down. He has commanded us to ". . . forgive, and ye shall be forgiven" (Luke 6:37).

Finally, the father gave a party for the prodigal, so he could share his joy with his friends. He knew the importance of surrounding the returning one with loving support and encouragement. "It is 'necessary' for us to make merry," the father explained to the boy's bitter brother. It was necessary, because the very angels rejoice in heaven over a sinner's repentance; and if heaven rejoices, we mortals have no option. True love rejoices over the *lost one that is found* and the *dead one that comes alive again.* And so this wise parent did the right thing.

Notice next how he dealt with his eldest son. I'm sure he realized that this wasn't going to be as easy. Somehow, it is an awful lot simpler to deal with the pigsty than to deal with the problem of pride. The prodigal prodigal is almost easier to love than the prodigal prig. I'm sure the father had been watching and waiting just as long a time for his oldest son to return to him, as he had for his youngest son. It wasn't that the boy's behavior had been anything but exemplary. There was no denying the fact that during the many long years of his brother's absence, he had borne the brunt of all the hard work and heavy responsibility that went with his position. He had been the *only* son for all that time, shouldering the overseeing of his father's estate. But the father was not stupid. The smoldering bitter resentment of his son's attitude had not been lost on him. He had deeply mourned the fact that his work had not been done thankfully or joyfully, and so was not taken aback when he was angrily confronted and accused of being a slavedriver.

"Lo, these many years do I serve thee . . ." (verse 29). Of course, this was not altogether true. The inheritance had been divided up between the brothers years ago. The older brother had not been slaving for his father at all, but rather for himself. But bitterness loses its perspective; jealousy tinges everything a dark, critical color. The father was so saddened to see the bitter spirit of judgment that was being displayed. Perhaps the younger son had dared to do the thing the older son had wanted to do all along. Who knows why such resentment festered and grew, but it was there—ready to flash out with a vicious protest at the first opportunity.

"This thy son was come, who hath devoured thy living with harlots . . ." (verse 30), he complained. Gently, the father began to reason with him. He loved that boy. He reminded him that his brother had come home, and it was therefore necessary that they celebrate. And then he told his son that even as his youngest son had never ceased to be a son, he had never stopped being a brother to him either. (There are some things that never change.) And then the father told his son that joyless service is really no service at all, and bitter obedience is a very poor substitute for glad duty rendered. The prodigal prig needed to be made fully aware he had never known what it was to truly serve, or to rightly rejoice, and was therefore in the most miserable state possible.

Prodigal prigs know very little about close relationships with their parents. Standing in the dusty road with their arms entwined around each other, heart beating against heart, father and younger son had been reconciled. But standing just outside the security of the family mansion, in the chilling cold of the eastern evening, the older brother could do nothing but complain about the distance in their relationship. He felt that his father had never spent enough time with him. He believed he had had a raw deal. "You never gave *me* a party," he pouted petulantly! "Son, thou art ever with me, and all that I have is thine," was the reply. But the son was thinking about a party—and not a parent! He was greedy and envious but had not put out the effort needed to improve his relationship with his father. What is more—pride forbade him to back down. Pride prevents a prodigal's penitence and that is very, very sad.

Tell me, do you have children who have never physically left home or church or the basic beliefs they have learned from their childhood days? Are they attending church and going through all the respectable motions of the upright, solid-citizen syndrome? And are they downright unhappy? Is there any joy in their religion, or evidence of sacrificial service? Is there a sense of real joy in their relationship with the family and with their God? Do they care about their brothers and their sisters? Do they look out for them? Have they watched with you from the housetop, or have they left you there alone? In other words, do you have a prodigal prig on your hands?

Not long ago, my husband went to Europe to speak at a missions conference. He noticed that the wife of one of the missionaries was listening very intently to what he had to say. At the end of the week's meetings, she came to talk with him and told him that she had been struggling with the assignment they had been given by their mission board. She had rebelled (though silently) about being sent to that particular field of service. "I remind me of my young son," she said ruefully. "He's always jumping up and down in church, and I'm always telling him to sit down, and be still. After one such battle of wills, he eventually sat down, but not before he had whispered in my ear: 'I'm sitting down on the outside, but I'm standing up on the inside!' "

I know what that honest lady meant. How often in my Christian service, God has discovered me sitting down on the outside, but standing up on the inside, refusing to budge in my obdurate attitude! Do you have a boy or a girl who is sitting down on the outside but is standing up on the inside? Or perhaps this describes your own attitude to the letter. It is at this point that we, as parents, must not fail. If we are prigs ourselves, demanding retribution for the suffering received at our children's hands, and refusing to go out of our way to reach our children, our child will in all probability never come in to the feast. Pride is a dastardly thing. God hates it. He tells us so in Proverbs 8:13. Pride refuses to say it's sorry, because it always believes it is right. Pride makes us feel superior and everyone else inferior. Pride provokes, pouts, preens and pushes people about. Pride is *never* penitent. We need to know also that pride is satanic in origin, and therefore needs to be recognized and dealt with. Pride was born when Lucifer said to himself, "I'm worth something apart from God, and I refuse to submit to anybody." Lucifer, father of the night, never says *he's* sorry, and he wants to make sure we don't say it either.

I will always remember the response of one of our sons, when Stuart apologized for making a wrong decision. Far from degrading himself in the child's eyes, I could instantly see that Dad's stock had risen sharply. And it opened the way for discussion, understanding, and a new warmth of fellowship between the two of them. If our children know that we fail, it helps them know that we are human, and also that they have freedom to make mistakes, too.

We don't confess our sins just because we've come to recognize the essence of sin is pride, and pride hurts the God we love; pride hurts us, too! It is just plain stupid to harbor a bitter spirit that will damage our personality. The father pled earnestly with the prodigal prig to be reconciled for his own good. "It is necessary that you come in and welcome your brother back," he insisted. It was necessary because an attitude of stubborn pride stunts the healthy growth of one's own Christian character. A root of bitterness that is not rooted out can begin to poison everything it touches. But pigheaded pride decides it isn't necessary to instigate anything from *its* side. It just waits around for the "enemy" to make a move before it makes itself vulnerable. Pride lets the sun go down on its wrath, and allows quick, hot anger and hurt to solidify into cold hatred that makes the heart as hard as concrete, as cold as ice, and as unforgiving as the devil himself.

If we refuse to forgive, we may become physically, emotionally, and socially sick. So if we can't be reconciled with our brother for God's sake, or *his* sake, surely we are selfish enough to be reconciled for our own sake.

When I became a Christian, someone gave me a little poem. It was written on a card, and as far as I can remember pointed out that the cross of Christ represented an *I* crossed out. At the foot of this symbol knelt a figure in the shape of a *C* praying, and underneath the picture were the words NOT I BUT CHRIST.

> Lord bend this strong and stiff-necked *I*—
> Help me to bow the neck and die—
> Beholding Him who died for me, on Calvary!

Jesus said that "except a corn of wheat fall into the ground and die, it abideth alone: but if it die, it bringeth forth much fruit" (John 12:24). The parent, prodigal, or the prig who refuses to die to all selfish considerations will find himself abiding alone. There will be no music, no fatted calf, and no feast for him. There will be neither robe, shoes, nor ring. There will be instead—lost loneliness, sore selfishness, biting bitterness, and failure that is failure indeed.

> Not I but Christ, be honored, loved, exalted;
> Not I, but Christ, be seen, be known, be heard;
> Not I, but Christ, in ev'ry look and action,
> Not I, but Christ, in ev'ry tho't and word.
>
> Not I but Christ, to gently soothe in sorrow;
> Not I, but Christ, to wipe the falling tear;
> Not I, but Christ, to lift the weary burden;
> Not I, but Christ, to hush away all fear.
>
> Christ, only Christ, no idle word e'er falling;
> Christ, only Christ, no needless bustling sound;
> Christ, only Christ, no self-important bearing;
> Christ, only Christ, no trace of "I" be found.

ADA A. WHIDDINGTON

WORKSHEET

Prodigal Prigs

Suggested time—15 minutes

1. Discuss or write a paragraph:
   a) With whom do you identify and why—the father, the prodigal prodigal, or the prodigal prig?
   b) Review the way the father dealt with his two sons. What did he do that helped you to see what you can do?
   c) What are some common mistakes we make when dealing with prodigal people?
   d) Are you a good forgiver?

Suggested time—10 minutes

2. Read 1 Corinthians 13:4–6. This is a description of the way love behaves. Make a list of these qualities. Take a few minutes and pray about one of these things.

Suggested time—5 minutes

3. Share an incident in your Christian life, when you have been sitting down on the outside but standing up on the inside.

Suggested time—15 minutes

4. "Pride do I hate, saith the Lord." Read the story of Nebuchadnezzar in Daniel, chapter 4 and discuss:
   a) The ways he was proud
   b) The things that happened to him
   c) The results of his humbling
   d) What do you learn from this?

Suggested time—5 minutes

5. Prayer Time
   Use the hymn at the end of the chapter as a prayer and/or pray spontaneously.

9

Blunt Believers

And the sons of the prophets said unto Elisha, Behold now, the place where we dwell with thee is too strait for us.

Let us go, we pray thee, unto Jordan, and take thence every man a beam, and let us make a place there, where we may dwell. And he answered, Go ye.

And one said, Be content, I pray thee, and go with thy servants. And he answered, I will go.

So he went with them. And when they came to Jordan, they cut down wood.

But as one was felling a beam, the axe head fell into the water: and he cried, and said, Alas, master! for it was borrowed.

And the man of God said, Where fell it? And he shewed him the place. And he cut down a stick, and cast it in thither; and the iron did swim.

Therefore said he, Take it up to thee. And he put out his hand, and took it.

2 Kings 6:1-7

A bout a man who thought he had a handle on things, but couldn't cut it!

Let me tell you about the situation. The man in question had been attending Elisha's Bible School. The seminary had been established by Elijah to instruct and train some of the most devout sons of Israel. In Elijah's day, the government of Israel headed up by compromising King Ahab and his heathen wife, Jezebel, had made things extremely difficult for the young prophets, and, at one point, had forced one hundred of them to hide out in a cave.

By the time Elisha succeeded Elijah, however, things seemed to be a little easier, with school enrollment up and expansion plans in progress. As the building program was about to commence, we find our young prophet enthusiastically borrowing an ax from a brother and setting off on a wood-chop. One of the students pressed Elisha to go with them, and he agreed. Finding a lovely site by the side of the river Jordan, they all set about clearing it.

"Let us go, let us build, let us dwell!" they cried, and so the work began.

Then it happened. As our young, dedicated (but, perhaps, inexperienced) woodsman flayed away at a trunk of a particularly tough tree, the most embarrassing thing occurred. The axhead flew right off the end of the handle and landed plumb in the middle of the river! He had literally lost his cutting edge—his sharpness, his effectiveness. It would obviously have been totally frustrating for him to continue hacking away at the tree with the handle of the ax. There

163

would certainly have been no discernible effect on the trees. That is for sure.

Now in the preceding chapters of this book, we have used many and varied pictures to describe the frustration of ineffective Christian living. In this chapter, I want to try to be practical about it all, and show you the steps to recovery.

Many Christians can identify with the shaggy sheep, the gripy grapes, the crumbling clay, or the pooped prophet. Perhaps there is no need to press the point any further. Enough to say that by now you are aware that possibly there is something wrong, but perhaps you don't quite know *how* to put it right! It's a bit like knowing you need Christ, but not understanding how to receive Him. It might be that you are totally frustrated (just like this young man who had been left with an outside job on his hands and only the handle of an ax to do it with). That's frustration. Maybe you have been landed with the youth work at your church. There's been nothing for the teenagers for years, but now someone has had the bright idea that you would be the ideal person for the job. The only problem is that you have never done anything with young people in your life, and you are now old enough to be their aging parent. You feel out of touch, helpless, and their music gives you a headache. But there is nothing wrong with your heart! You love the Lord, want to build His Kingdom, and decide to have a go. After trying everything you can think of, however, nothing seems to have worked. The kids are lethargic, you are bored with your own lessons, and the whole project appears to be an exercise in futility. I'm sure if something like this is the case, then you can fully identify with this young man who tried to get a handle on the situation but found he couldn't cut it. But wait a minute! If you are discouraged, it may not be a question of an error of judgment on your part: ("I shouldn't have taken it on in the first place."). It may simply be a matter of working in the flesh instead of the Spirit. It's most important that you find out exactly what *is* wrong, because there could just be a simple remedy—especially if you can look back to the start of the project, and remember that things went really well at the beginning. I am sure if this is the case our young hero can help you. It may be that, like him, you have simply lost the cutting edge of your Christianity. Let's see how the young man coped with his dilemma.

After frustration came contemplation. He stopped flailing away at the trees with the handle of the ax, and gave some serious thought to the matter. This is always a wise thing to do, as I have observed many Christians go on, trying to cut down the trees, knowing full well that their axes are blunt. That's one reason we have kids battered and dented by their Sunday-school teachers, evangelists preaching to empty pews, and youth workers having nervous breakdowns. People will not stop their manifold activities and ask questions, but just keep right on going. Now I'm not advocating packing in a job in midstream. There is far too much of that going on as it is, but I *am* suggesting a fierce inner honesty, as we try to grapple with the situation. Notice next that our young Bible student did not do his contemplating alone.

"Alas, master!" he cried. To whom did he cry? He cried to Elisha, the mighty prophet. He certainly went to the right person for his answer. We need to look around carefully as we seek help and ask ourselves:

Can we really trust this man we have turned to for help, or this woman we have confided in? Do they know God? Have they been born again? Are they sound in doctrine? Do they believe that the Bible is the inspired Word of God, and that Jesus Christ is God's Son?

There are an awful lot of cultic counselors prowling around in the woods, watching out for frustrated Bible students. Each one is well equipped to offer quick spiritual fixes for our problems. When the time comes to get advice, make sure you go to the right person for it. Pray about that. Ask God to protect you—especially if you are a new believer. Implore the Holy Spirit to alert you to heretical advice that is not rooted and grounded firmly in the Scriptures.

I can think of a time when I was a very ignorant, young Christian and needed a whole bunch of questions answered. Some were doctrinal and some were about such matters as failure, dryness, fruitlessness, and bluntness. Well aware that I was naive and vulnerable, I wondered how ever I was going to be able to discern between truth and error. About that time I heard about the training British banks gave their inspectors to help them spot counterfeit bills. I would have thought they should have shut the men up with a whole heap of phony money, so they could have learned what it looked like. Instead, they put the trainees in a vault full of genuine currency for a week and told them to count it. At the end of this time, they slipped a few counterfeit bills amongst the cash. They were detected immediately. I realized that I had to *soak* myself in the Bible at a fast rate. I needed to make up for lost time and catch up, counting the spiritual wealth that was laid up for me in the vaults of Scripture; and *then* I had to trust God to help me to recognize the counterfeit notes. The way to stay straight on doctrine isn't to study all the weird cults and heresies that are abroad; but rather to make sure we are furiously counting the real thing, until we become full-fledged inspectors.

The young prophet had chosen the right Bible program and had a great teacher to help him become adept at all the skills involved in his profession; when he had a problem he knew he could go straight to God's man and trust him. So what was his plea, once he had found his wise counselor?

"Alas, master," he said, "I've lost it!" Now, even though he was fortunate to have wise counsel at hand, that still must have been a pretty difficult thing to admit to. When you think about it, he must have felt pretty dumb. I'm sure pride is one of the main stumbling blocks that prevents us from seeking answers for our spiritual bluntness. We think about how stupid we are going to look, showing Elisha the "handle."

Once I found myself prevented from asking for help for just this very reason. When I was a full-time Christian youth worker, I couldn't see how I could admit that I had a problem. Certainly I didn't feel I could tell my superior. Anyway, I thought I wasn't supposed to have *any* problems, and I didn't want her to know about it because I felt she might despise me—or worse still—remove me from my position. I was sure it would be better to just keep very quiet and say nothing. I reasoned that if I did go and talk it over with her, she was bound to tell me I was expected to sort it out myself, and so nothing would be gained. I had already discov-

ered that when you have been given a position of authority, everyone expects you to know everything about everything. Pastors'
wives are expected to know everything their husbands know, for
example, so it's hard for any of us in leadership to come to the point
of saying, "I don't know the answer."

Our young man however had no such problem. Perhaps the fact
that the ax had been borrowed had something to do with that. He
knew that his loss deeply affected another person. The iron tool had
been lent to him, and this happened in a community where such
precious implements were valuable possessions, indeed. Perhaps it
is this realization above all others that eventually drives most of us
to someone for help. We see our families beginning to feel the effect
of our bluntness. Our husband, our children, or perhaps the committee we work with at the church, sense our frustration. For a long
time I believed that no one needed to know I had lost the axhead. (I
reckoned it was nobody's business but mine anyway.) But there
came a time when I had to admit that there was nothing getting
built around the clearing by the river; and I really did care about
those dearest to me who were being affected by my edgeless life,
which was bruising *their* personalities. It was at this point, and for
this reason, I decided it was time to ask for help.

Elisha calmly confronted the young man and asked him a very
straightforward question. "Where fell it?" (Let's retrace your steps,
he suggested, and see if we can identify the place you lost your effectiveness.) Now that is a really practical suggestion. When we
know we've *lost* it, and have decided we want to *find* it, we must try
to retrace our steps.

I am a notorious loser of keys. Every time I have been somewhere
in the car, I forget to hang the keys up on the pretty wooden plaque
by our backdoor, designed for that purpose. I put those keys down
someplace, and forget about them until it's time to go somewhere
else. Then—*panic!* Over and over again, my long-suffering husband
has had to take me by the arm and gently ask me, "Where did you
go when you first came into the house? Let's retrace your steps."
Sure enough, as I think back to the time I had the keys, and pains-
takingly retrace my steps until the moment that I lost them, I find

them again. There they are hanging on the kitchen cabinet, lying on a book, or even snuggled among the laundry at the bottom of the laundry basket. You have to start by asking yourself that all-important question: "Where fell it?"

Before we go on, however, just what are we talking about when we say we can lose our *cutting edge?* We are really describing the difference between a life of Spirit-filled activity; one that gets God's Kingdom built and makes an indelible impression for Him; and a self-filled life of carnal activity that doesn't do any of those things. We can expend enormous amounts of energy being busily ineffective, because we've somehow crossed over that fine line from being a spiritual man to being a carnal one. Let me define some terms for you. A *natural* man is a man without any spiritual life. He has not been born from above. He behaves as a natural man must, being captivated, motivated, and activated by himself. A *spiritual* man is a natural man who has received the life of the Spirit and is captivated, motivated, and activated by God. His thoughts and activities demonstrate that fact, and everyone around him benefits. According to my husband's definition: *a carnal man is a spiritual man who lives like a natural man.* He tries to cut down the trees with the handle of his ax. He works terribly hard for God but gets nowhere, and everyone watches him become more and more exhausted and frustrated. Once we yield to the Lordship of Christ (which may or may not be a "crisis" experience for us), we must continue the process of yielding to His control on an ongoing moment-by-moment basis. So it is we can be spiritually sharp and effective one day, but carnal and blunt the next. Practicing the Presence of God or the controlling Lordship of Christ, enables us to grow adept at recognizing just when we've lost our edge. Losing the axhead does not mean we can lose Christ, or that the Holy Spirit flies off us, according to our behavior, but it does mean the difference between cutting down the trees edged by His power, and making little impression in the woods at all.

Now we can lose His control, and with it, the edge or the axhead at 1001 different places! We have already suggested some of these points in the preceding chapters, so let me just remind you of a few of them. It could have been by the river of carelessness, busy-ness, worldliness, selfishness, stubbornness, or prayerlessness, that the axhead has fallen. Or it could be lost in a stream we haven't even got around to mentioning.

I can think of times that I have faithfully prayed for my children. An awareness that they have not been among the most positive of peers has sent me to my knees. But then the danger has passed, and I have quickly grown careless. The fact that I have not seen the prowling wolf has not meant that the animal has not been there. As I have grown careless in my attitude and blasé in my complacency, I have ceased to pray effectively for my child. I have also been in danger of losing my sharpness by the river of worldliness. Because I am a woman who is married to a well-known Bible teacher, and has been gifted with certain speaking abilities, I am given many opportunities to be up front—on stage—in view. I love being the woman God made me to be, but I have to watch my whole attitude in this regard. If I am not careful, I can accept invitations that women have not had the opportunity to take before, just to show folk a woman can do it. At that point I am in danger of losing my effectiveness.

We have to identify the exact place we cease to be sharp. God will help us to do that if we get alone with Him, or counsel with an Elisha. As we thoughtfully retrace our steps and ask ourselves when things were all right, and then when things went all wrong, we should be able to identify the problem.

I remember sitting on a plane bound for California on my way to speak at a ladies' retreat. It had been hard to board that plane for many reasons. First of all, I didn't like leaving the family to fend for themselves, even though everything I could have done to make it easy and light had been done. The fridge was lost under mounds of paper, all with explicit instructions, maps, telephone numbers, smile faces, reminders of my love, and even a dollar or two "in case" money for each child! Yet I didn't have the faith to believe they would even bother reading any of it, and wondered if they would survive at all till I returned. Then there was the little matter of the plane I had boarded. I didn't know they still had such ancient airbirds in service. I was sure the pilot had a calendar in the cockpit, instead of a watch, but that was most probably because I was so nervous, each minute seemed like an hour. Glancing down the aisle, I was not a little concerned to observe how the passengers were seated. Hoping no one would notice, I surreptitiously slipped into an aisle seat to "balance things up a bit." I didn't have the faith to believe that that plane would hold me up or get me to my destination on time. Then I was worried about my mother. She was not well, and since she lived in England, I felt helpless, being in the USA. I didn't have the faith to believe that she was in the best of hands, or that I was being told the full story.

Seeking to drag myself away from such dark forebodings, I fished in my bag and took out my notes. I decided to go over the talk that I would be giving in a few short hours. Opening my Bible at the appropriate passage, I glanced at the heading of my address **FAITH**. Immobilized with conviction, I realized something had to be done between *now* and *then,* if I were not to arrive with the handle of the ax and very little else! A wave of fear had swallowed up my effectiveness, and I had little trouble identifying the place!

Once the young man had shown Elisha just where the axhead had been lost, the man of God did the strangest thing. Breaking a stick off one of the overhanging branches, he applied the wood to the exact place indicated by the young man. What a graphic illustration of the cross being applied to the area of our need! Christ died to make us fit for heaven and lives to make us fit for earth. We have to make the application of His death and Resurrection to the place of our failure. If we are to recover our usefulness, we need to realize Christ can do something about it, and will intervene on our behalf. He died for the sins of our carelessness, busy-ness, stubbornness, and worldliness. He lives to forgive and cleanse us from them. We need to apply that forgiveness to the explicit point of our failure. We can then say that we are sorry, repent, and claim His promise to give us the power to be different.

Way down beside the River Jordan, a miracle happened. The application of the wood had caused the iron to swim. In other words, it brought back the axhead within reach. The death and life of Christ can restore our cutting edge. No matter at which point we lose it, He can bring the whole glorious possibility of a Christian life that works well back into sight. Yes, He can!

Elisha told the young man exactly what to do next. Having known frustration, and engaged in contemplation, he was now instructed in the art of appropriation.

"Take it up to thee," commanded the prophet. "And he put out his hand and took it." What a thrilling concept. Some of us having lived with failure most of our Christian lives, have settled down to a state of mediocrity, deciding that a handle without a head is apparently all that there is to the Christian life. If that is your case—*listen up!* "Take it up to thee," commands your heavenly Elisha. There *is* something you can do to retrieve your edge. There is something *He* will do that we cannot; and there is something *we* must do that He will not! He will bring the sharp possibilities into sight—but we need to begin to see the possibility as a probability. We have to say: "I *will* believe I can be God's man [or woman] in God's world, building God's Kingdom God's way—pleasing my Lord, blessing my kids, effectively serving Him; I *will*, I *will* believe!"

Then we have to start to live as if we believe it, even before we do. We will need to go to our minister and ask for that job we didn't think we could manage. We will have to get going, as if we were cutting it already; and as we move ahead, trusting Him for His enabling—working not in our own strength but in His—then the trees will begin to fall!

The problem with failure is the sense of finality it can produce. If you have had a really bad tumble, and fallen down in full view of everybody, it is the hardest thing in the world to believe there is any hope for the future. There was a time in my experience when I really felt I had failed to keep the home fires burning. Seeking to be Mom and Dad to three rambunctious children, I had come to the end of my resources, and ended up in the hospital with a bleeding ulcer. The depression I endured at that time had more to do with a bleeding heart than a bleeding stomach. I had failed to cope. Here was my good husband laboring for the Lord, and here *I* was falling down on the job at home. The children were getting out of hand, schoolwork assignments were not being completed, and their behavior patterns showed alarming trends. And now I had worried myself into the hospital. Where was all that faith I had talked so long and so loudly about?

"Christians don't get ulcers," a well-meaning friend admonished me, looking at me very severely. I was sure she was right. How could I face my fellow workers, and more importantly my Bible class—and most important of all—my children, and tell them I had an ulcer! It was not until a beautiful feminine counterpart of the Mighty Prophet visited me, and laughed me out of my despondency, that I was able to be objective again.

"Why Jill," my friend teased me, "with the load you carry, you should have ten ulcers! You must be growing in grace to have only one!"

"But what do I do about the problems at home?" I wailed.

"Get better as quickly as you can, and get yourself back to those kids of yours. They're missing you like crazy," she answered. "Start over, regroup, drop some commitments, trust the Lord to work it out, and if anyone says anything so stupid to you again about Christians not having ulcers, refer them to the apostle Paul's thorn in the flesh; for all we know, that could have been an ulcer too. Christians are bound to get sick, like anyone else, and if it's a sickness related to worry, just think how much sicker you would be if you'd never found Christ at all!"

In essence, my friend helped me to remember that failure is never final. It's hard to remember, when you're down physically and have blown it spiritually; when you are wiped out emotionally and feel ostracized socially; but that's the very time you need to say cheerfully to the world in general, and your accusers in particular: "Christians aren't *made*—they are in the making!" Then bend down to the water's edge, and having applied the cross, watch the iron swim up into sight! Pick it up, "Take it up to thee"; then dry your tears and wash your face—and get on with it!

In the end, the way in which we shall know whether we are living carnal or spiritual lives is by the measure of our effectiveness. Notice, I carefully didn't say *successful* Christian life; I said *effective!* I can witness to someone and be effective in the sense that he understands my presentation of the Gospel, and is deeply convicted by it. This is not to say that he will respond and be successfully converted. But if the axhead is in place, then the message will be thoroughly conveyed, cutting deep into his soul, and he will know that it is true. Progress will eventually be seen, and the trees will topple over at last—*if* we continue felling them in His power. I'm quite sure it took many, many swings of that axhead before the trees eventually hit the dust; and it will probably take a similarly long time before we are able to cut through all the bark and timber necessary to accomplish God's way in a life. But the power to continue, the physical endurance, and the tough-minded determination to keep swinging—this—*this* will be our experience! He promises it will be so!

Consider rearing children, for example. How many a mother looks despairingly around a quarrelsome threesome, picking and clawing at each other over some trivial thing, and hopes against hope it's not the pastor at the door. It takes a spiritual mother, indeed, to keep chipping away at all that sort of family forestry. Even though that rough and tumble is perfectly normal, it can be dreadfully depressing; and it can tempt us to think we have failed to produce the sweet little angelic beings we believed, as Christian parents, we should be rearing! The power to keep hacking away at the undergrowth comes from appropriating God's gracious resources.

As the young prophet put out his hand and took the iron to him again, he must have rejoiced. Having known frustration, engaged in contemplation, learned the art of appropriation, he finished up in exultation. There is nothing quite like the thrill of calling out at the top of one's lungs: *"Timber!"* Which of us who has worked with students does not know that lift of spirit, when a bright boy or girl (who has resisted us for months), finally finds that last argument cut away, all their excuses chopped down, and is felled at the feet of Jesus! *Exultation* is the only word for that. Which of us, after months of swinging at the prehistoric children's program of our church, has had the joy of axing away the old dead wood? How many times have you seen a clearing made in a shaded glade of an elder's or a deacon's mind, when for years they haven't been able to see the wood for the trees? Exultation!

As we appropriate the power of the Spirit, we have the chance to be effective for Him. So—where fell it? Identify the place, apply the cross, see the iron swim, and "Take it up to thee." Let's get going and get this house built!

> Failure in my walk and witness,
>   Failure in my work I see;
> Fruitless toil, un-Christlike living,
>   Calling forth no praise to Thee.
>
> Now to Thee my soul confesses
>   All its failure, all its sin;
> All the pride, the self-contentment,
>   All the "secret faults" within.
>
> Save me from myself, my Father,
>   From each subtle form of pride;
> Lead me now with Christ to Calvary,
>   Show me I with Him have died.
>
> No more let it be my working,
>   Nor my wisdom, love, or power,
> But the life of Jesus only,
>   Passing through me hour by hour.
>
> Let the fulness of Thy Spirit
>   Resting on Him cover me,
> That the witness borne to others,
>   May bring glory, Lord, to Thee.
>
>   FREDA H. ALLEN

WORKSHEET

Blunt Believers

Suggested time—5 minutes

1. Define a *natural* man; a *spiritual* man; and *carnal* man.

Suggested time—20 minutes

2. Read Romans 8:1–17
   (If you are working on your own, fill in the answers in your notebook.)
   a) If you are working in a group, split up into threes and read five verses each until you get to verse 17.
   b) Let each person collect information from these verses under the following headings (and try to put your findings into your own words).

The Natural Man	*The Spiritual Man*	*The Carnal Man*
Example: verse 5—thinks only natural thoughts	verse 6—has life and peace	verse 6—is dead

Suggested time—5 minutes

3. Share your discoveries within the small group of three, or with the larger class.

Suggested time—10 minutes

4. Discuss the following steps to the recovery of the lost axhead:
   a) identifying the place
   b) applying the wood
   c) putting out our hand and retrieving the axhead

Suggested time—5 minutes

5. According to the above, where do you see yourself at this time?

Suggested time—5 minutes

6. Prayer Time
   Use the hymn at the end of the chapter as a prayer, or pray
   spontaneously.

10

Hindered Harriers

In Gibeon the Lord appeared to Solomon in a dream by night: and God said, Ask what I shall give thee.

And Solomon said, Thou hast shewed unto thy servant David my father great mercy, according as he walked before thee in truth, and in righteousness, and in uprightness of heart with thee; and thou has kept for him this great kindness, that thou hast given him a son to sit on his throne, as it is this day.

And now, O Lord my God, thou hast made thy servant king instead of David my father: and I am but a little child: I know not how to go out or come in.

And thy servant is in the midst of thy people which thou hast chosen, a great people, that cannot be numbered nor counted for multitude.

Give therefore thy servant an understanding heart to judge thy people, that I may discern between good and bad: for who is able to judge this thy so great a people?

And the speech pleased the Lord, that Solomon had asked this thing.

And God said unto him, Because thou hast asked this thing, and hast not asked for thyself long life; neither hast asked riches for thyself, nor hast asked the life of thine enemies; but hast asked for thyself understanding to discern judgment;

Behold, I have done according to thy words: lo, I have given thee a wise and an understanding heart; so that there was none like thee before thee, neither after thee shall any arise like unto thee.

And I have also given thee that which thou hast not asked, both riches, and honour: so that there shall not be any among the kings like unto thee all thy days.

And if thou wilt walk in my ways, to keep my statutes and my commandments, as thy father David did walk, then I will lengthen thy days.

1 Kings 3:5-14

In the end, the bottom line is the finishing line.

Someone has said, "It's not the way a man starts his Christian life that matters—but how he finishes it that counts." It *all* counts, of course, but I understand the sense of that statement. Solomon started the race of life with everything going for him, but was tripped up on the track. He ran absolutely superbly for twenty long and glorious laps, and then slipped to the back of the pack—thereby, losing the prize well before the finishing post was even in sight. As far as God's purposes and pleasure was concerned, Solomon lost the race.

Paul likened the Christian life to a race with a prize at the end of it. He talked about his own involvement, fearing he should ". . . run, in vain" (Galatians 2:2). He told the Corinthians that ". . . they which run in a race run all, but one receiveth the prize . . ." and then exhorted them to "So run, that ye may obtain" (1 Corinthians 9:24). In Philippians 3:14 he told the believers that he pressed "toward the mark for the prize of the high calling of God in Christ Jesus," and at the end of his life was able to tell Timothy, his spiritual son in the faith, that he had ". . . finished his course" (2 Timothy 4:7). Writing to the "foolish Galatians" (Galatians 3:1), he chided them saying, "Ye did run well; who did hinder you that ye should not obey the truth?" (5:7). If Paul had been alive at the end of Solomon's days, he may well have asked the king the same question.

Meeting Solomon at the very beginning of his reign we cannot help but be impressed with the young man. What catches our attention is the fact that God's blessings were bestowed upon him in such a liberal manner. He appears to be one of God's favorite people! We may wonder about this, until we read about his prayer life. If you searched the Scriptures for a man who prayed prayers that pleased God, you would not need to go past 1 Kings 3. For an example: One night God walked into Solomon's dream and asked, ". . . what shall I give thee?" (verse 5). What an opportunity! This is the stuff that fairy tales are made of. Can you possibly imagine what it would be like to have God visit you in this manner? What would your answer be, if you were told you could have anything in the world you wanted? God wanted to please Solomon, and Solomon ended up pleasing God. The young king's prayer certainly bears examination, not just because we all want to know how to pray prayers that please God, but also because it tells us much about Solomon's character and the excellent start to the race that he ran.

Our prayer life plays a vital part in forming our Christian character, and I also believe that the effectiveness of our ministry, whether we be pastor, pastor's wife, Sunday-school teacher, secretary or choir member, depends upon the quality of our prayer life, too. Do you remember, in the story of the brittle bones in the dry valley, that God's prophet Ezekiel preached until the isolated bones came back together again, and the flesh, sinews and skin covered the skeletons, and yet there was still no life in them? It took the powerful God-directed praying of Ezekiel to unlock that blessing, so those Israeli corpses could stand up upon their feet. In the light of this and the example of Solomon, we need to think about our prayer life in a little deeper detail.

There seem to be two common attitudes abroad today concerning prayer. One can be summed up very simply by saying, "There is too little of it," and the other by saying, "There is too much." The first problem is one of complacency. If you are blessed (as we are in our church fellowship, with an excellent prayer committee), you will know there is a great temptation to leave it all to them! After all, we believe in the diversity of gifts in the Body of Christ, so why not leave all the praying to the prayer committee members who apparently must have discovered their gift, because that's why they are doing it. So goes the argument.

That is a bit like leaving the winning of the race to the most gifted runners. As I watched cross-country races, I learned that as much depended upon Number 6 in the pack as did upon the up-front runners with the speed. Oftentimes we leave it to the prayer committee, forgetting the team concept that is absolutely necessary to win the race. We also get off the hook this way, so we can concentrate on all the active things we like to do, instead of the passive pastime of prayer. Now there are problems with that way of thinking. First of all, we cannot afford to complacently think that prayer is a gift. Prayer is the means by which we communicate with God, and while the opportunity to do that has been won for us by the Lord Jesus and His gift of salvation, prayer itself is not a spiritual gift, as such. It is not intended for a spiritual elite, who likes that sort of thing, and it is not an optional extra either, but rather a *must* for every child of God, and especially for the one who has been entrusted with the responsibility of leading others. Leaders do not start as learners on a ladder, the bottom rung of which is called "prayer," and graduate upwards to speaking and teaching, leaving their prayers behind them. Rather, leaders need to learn to pray with even more expertise, as they climb into more complicated areas of service. We must not leave it to the prayer committee. It is very nice, indeed, to have a prayer committee, a prayer chain, prayer partners, prayer breakfasts, and anything else that will teach, help, and encourage God's people to pray—but we mustn't treat them like the Holy Spirit, running to them as the first need arises that *they* might bear our problems before the throne. We must learn to first take our own needs to God, and then and only then, share them with the prayer committee. *Faith* is the spiritual gift that can be exercised through the medium of prayer. There is no doubting the fact that a few of God's choicest servants have this ministry of faith, and exercise it on behalf of others through the medium of prayer. But that doesn't change the fact that all of us need to be our *own* prayer committee. The Lord Jesus commanded us to pray, and did not say to His disciples *if* you pray, but rather *when* you pray (Matthew 6:5).

For the committed Christian then, prayer is a necessity, and we find Solomon fully conversant with this fact. We also find him avoiding another trap we often fall into—that of believing prayer is only for the elderly. Leave it to the retired Christians in the old folks' home, we say, as we get on with our prayerless Christian service in the name of the Lord.

If prayer was intended only for the elderly, how was it that Jesus Christ at the age of thirty-three was an expert at it? We have no idea how old we shall be before we go to heaven, and wouldn't it be a shame to arrive there and not know what to say? After all, those who have been communicating with the Lord well down here will not be lost for words up there!

Solomon did not believe that prayer was for the pacifist either. A battle was raging within the young king's heart, concerning the great task he had been given, and his prayer experience was a wrestling and not a resting thing. By the very nature of their personalities, leaders are usually activists, and it is hard for such people to be still, to sit down to meditate or pray. But the fact that we think prayer is always passive is another misconception. Some aspects of prayer are undoubtedly passive. Remember the sheep, resting beside the still waters in the shepherd's psalm? There is a beautiful picture of the passive side of prayer, but there are many verses that give us other light on the subject altogether. What about the verse that says, "We wrestle not against flesh and blood, but against principalities, against powers, against the rulers of the darkness of this world, against spiritual wickedness in high places" (Ephesians 6:12).

This sort of praying doesn't sound very passive to me. Corrie ten Boom loved to exhort her audiences to *nestle,* rather than to *wrestle,* but she was referring to "trust and the rest of faith" and, in fact, engaged in much personal prayer warfare herself during her lifelong ministry. *KOKTD,* she would tell us cheerfully, which means of course, "Keep on kicking the devil," and what better way to do that than through believing prayer? As the old adage puts it, "The devil trembles when he sees the weakest saint upon his knees." What then does he do when he sees the strongest ones getting down to pray?

I well remember rushing to complete a Bible study I had been preparing for a group of rather wild teenagers. Not having much time, I tried to figure out which was the most important thing to do—prepare or pray. Both were important, but my time was so limited. I decided I had better prepare *myself* first, and then use the rest of the time to prepare my message. I discovered that preparing ourselves to prepare our messages makes for powerful preaching. Preaching a message, however well prepared, without preparing ourselves, is like running a race without working out! If you do that, you find you run out of steam, make a fool of yourself, or let the team down.

I think one of the most common reasons we pray so little is the cost of it. Not too many of us are willing to go beyond the *point of push.*

Let me illustrate this. I jog. I have not always been a runner, but our two oldest children ran on the cross-country team for their high school, and I began to run around the course, trying to keep up to cheer them on. Finding I enjoyed this, I began to walk a few miles every day, and about half-way round the course I had set myself, I suddenly thought of all the things that needed to be done at home. So I simply decided to hurry back. To my surprise, I found I could keep going, and so began my experience with jogging. After I bought a good pair of shoes and got into running on a regular basis, I discovered an interesting thing. There was a *point of push,* when I seemed to meet a sort of barrier that I needed to get through. This required extra effort, just when I didn't have any left. Just before I reached this point, all I wanted to do was quit. Totally out of breath, with my legs feeling like weights, I just *knew* I had to stop. It was at that very *point of push* that one day I jogged on—and found myself through that unseen barrier and out the other side. Once there, I discovered myself strong enough to run another ten miles, if necessary, and what's more—enjoy it! The sad thing is that prayer can be like this, with the majority of folk living their lives *this* side of the barrier. They never get through to the other side and there-fore never finish the course. They quit at the point of push. Up they get from the side of their beds after their morning quiet time, won-dering, what's so great about prayer anyway? Next time this hap-pens to you, stay still at your bedside—jog on—and you'll be through to a whole new dimension of intercession. It is all waiting for you, just the other side of the barrier. You'll see.

And so complacency, or a misconception of prayer, or the very effort that it takes to enjoy the experience, stops us from going on—pressing toward the mark, as Paul put it. That's a great pity. The Scripture calls someone whose Christianity costs him nothing a *carnal Christian.* Carnal Christians don't pray much. The little they pray amounts to the quick-fix variety, and does little damage to the evil one and little good to others. I heard about a seminar that was being offered that suggested there was a way to get a whole day's praying into ten minutes! In our "instant" society, I'm sure the ap-plications for that particular workshop flooded in.

I think we will all agree that there is far too little praying going on. But then we have the other extreme, too. There is far too much, as well. "What do you mean," you ask? "How can there be too much, when you've just spent all this time telling us there is too lit-tle?" It is true that there can never be too much of the right thing, but then there surely can be too much of the wrong thing. Listen to Jesus saying, "When thou prayest, thou shalt not be as the hypo-crites are: for they love to pray . . . (Matthew 6:5). Hypocrites "love to pray." How about that? How is it that hypocrites and heathens love to pray but Christians don't? Well, Jesus is not talking about *communication with God,* but is dealing with *communication with man.* He is talking about public praying—loud talk, or play acting. In another passage of Scripture, He tells us about a Pharisee who prayed thus "with himself" and said, "God, I thank thee that I am not as other men are, extortioners, unjust, adulterers, or even as this publican [tax collector]. I fast twice in the week, I give tithes of all that I possess" (Luke 18:11, 12). He was his own god and addressed his prayers to himself.

The hypocrite prays to others, hoping to make a great impression upon them with his false piety. There is far too much of this sort of praying going on, *even in the church.* People can pray in a church prayer meeting "like the heathen do" with needless repetitions, having their thoughts sadly upon other members of the group, instead of on their God. Or they may use up all the prayer requests before anyone else has a chance to use even one of them. I'm sure many of us can identify with the circle of chairs, the list of prayer requests, and the pounding heart as the public pray-ers get through the list like locusts, leaving nothing for those of us who are at the edge of the circle. Jesus tells us people like this think they will be heard for their much speaking. So that sort of praying is *too much* of the wrong sort of praying.

So then, how can we pray prayers that truly please God? Where is our model? There is a model right here in the Book of Kings in the person of young King Solomon. Successor to his father, David, King of Israel, the Scriptures tell us that "the speech that Solomon prayed pleased the Lord" (*see* 1 Kings 3:10). Now we have been given a clue. We see that the secret of praying effective prayers lies in the *what* we ask for. What were the requests that Solomon made? Well, before we look at what he did ask for, let's look at what he *didn't* request.

We catch the sense of God's joy in all of this. He is so happy that Solomon didn't ask for the usual things. Have you decided yet what you would have asked for if God appeared in your dreams and gave you a choice? I wonder if you would have asked for health, wealth, or security? I believe if Solomon had asked for any of these things, God would have granted them. But he didn't. He didn't even mention his health, or his wealth, or his enemies. I have to confess to spending an inordinate amount of prayer time asking God about my health. Don't you? All our aches and pains are carefully cataloged for God, as if He wasn't aware of their existence. We want to live just as long as anyone else has ever managed to live, and we can use up all our prayer time to that end. God was pleased with Solomon because his mind was on other people and *their* health and well-being, rather than on his own. It has been said that what you eat you are, or what you dress you are, but I believe fervently that what you *pray,* you are—and Solomon showed publicly what he was privately.

Solomon didn't pray about wealth either. Now this really pleased the heart of God. If we are not busy praying about our health, we are probably busy praying about our wealth! As Christians, we can get so caught up with the budget or money matters to the exclusion of everything else! "Neither hast [thou] asked riches for thyself," said God approvingly. The Lord has promised to provide for our needs, and if we will seek God's plan for our lives, we can trust Him to provide for them. Solomon didn't concern himself with his enemies either. It would have been understandable if the young king had spent his wish on his enemies. He could have wiped them off the face of the earth if he had wanted to, but he didn't want to. He followed the path of peace, and let God take care of his enemies for him. As Christians, we spend such a few precious moments in prayer, we need to spend them praying about other than our health, wealth, and our enemies!

We've talked about what Solomon didn't pray for, but what then did he ask? First of all, he prayed for the maturity he would need to do the job that God had given him to do. "I am but a little child," he said. He prayed for a wise and understanding heart and discernment to know the right and wrong of a matter, and he prayed about the hopeless feeling of inadequacy that he felt as he prepared to step into his father's shoes. Can you imagine what he was experiencing, as he prepared to take over his father's kingdom? "I know not how to go out or come in," he cried in fright. Numbers 27:15–17 and 2 Samuel 5:1, 2 use the phrase *to go out and come in* in relation to King David himself. The verses talk of David as shepherd and warrior, who led and protected and fought for his people Israel. In the face of his father's incredible gifts and worldwide reputation, young Solomon nearly quit before the gun went off. He thought that having to live up to all that was impossible. He just couldn't believe that he could be like his father.

Being interested in cross-country running has brought us into contact with many families. There is a high school in our conference that has been a constant competitor with our children's team.

For eight years or so, there has been a name that strikes fear into any high schooler's cross-country heart—*Stintzi!* This family of Stintzis seems to go on forever. Every season there has been one and sometimes two members of that family, flashing past the finishing line, ahead of every child in every school in the district. They are a family of fabulous runners. But can't you see the pressure there could be in that family? How could you break the line of succession and play tennis or soccer, instead of going out for cross-country? I'm sure there must have been struggles in those children's lives as they have sought to emulate their brother runner ahead of them. Thus it was with Solomon. Just how was he to run the race after his father's reputation had spread the wide world over?

But the Lord delights to hear the prayers of inadequacy—those requests that speak of our desperate need of Him. The one who prays in humility is heard loud and clear in the heavenlies. God delights, not only to hear such prayers, but to answer them. He loves to lean out of heaven and assure us that He has not made us like King David, but He has made us like *us.* He told Solomon that He would give him a wise and discerning heart because He had made him king in place of his father, David, and therefore had every intention of giving him the tools to finish the job. David, in fact, had been prevented from building the temple because his hands were stained with blood, but not so Solomon. He would be the one to build the splendid earthly dwelling place for Jehovah, which David would never even see.

The frightening sense of total inadequacy that young King Solomon voiced was a prayer that God would delight to answer, as He helped the young king to grow into total dependency upon Him.

Not long ago, I was due to speak to a seminar in Dallas, Texas. As I looked over the correspondence it chilled my bones. *Big D and little me,* I thought. The reason I had a severe dose of inadequacy was simply because I felt threatened by "ultrasuede" ladies. I have written about this problem in other books, but that is not to say that the battle, won once, means the battle always won. Opportunities to fail often appear from the very areas we thought we had a handle on. After all, the Scripture warns us: "Let him that thinketh he standeth take heed lest he fall" (1 Corinthians 10:12). As I prepared, I tried to encourage my heart with lessons learned in the past. I had run this particular race before—and won it. Surely I could do it again. It didn't help when people kept telling me how many seminars had preceded mine. Each one had been led by a "super girl," who (I was told) knew exactly how to dress, communicate, and charm those ultrasuede ladies! Praying about it, and searching for some word of exhortation from the Scriptures, I came across the verse that said ". . . man looketh on the outward appearance, but the Lord looketh on the heart" (1 Samuel 16:7). What really matters, God was saying, is that you are ultrasuede on the *inside*. Now that I could handle! Kneeling at His feet, I was happy to let Him dress my Spirit and then I knew I was ready for Big *D!*

Have you ever felt like that? Perhaps you are taking over as president of the women's society in your church fellowship, and you are following the most efficient president in the history of the church; or maybe you are a pastor's kid, and the whole world seems to expect you to turn out as a carbon copy of your dad; or then again you may have been given a spiritual assignment that has set you down in the midst of a teeming multitude of people, and *you* are expected to have the wisdom and discernment to govern them! Do you identify with Solomon? I'm sure you do.

Notice carefully the way that Solomon began to pray about all those things. He didn't pray, "Get me out of this," or, "Here am I, send somebody else," or, "Make me like my dad." He prayed, "Give me the tools and I'll finish the job!" He asked, as the little child that he knew that he was, in face of the huge task that lay before him, that his Heavenly Father would provide the necessary discernment, knowledge, and judgment he would need. He leaned upon his Lord and found that He was, indeed, the Coach and Captain. He discovered, as the apostle Paul did, that "Faithful is he that calleth you, who also will do it" (1 Thessalonians 5:24). God assured him, "[Because thou] hast asked for thyself understanding to discern judgment, Behold I have done according to thy words . . ." (1 Kings 3:11, 12). Remember the clay yielding its shape to the Potter's wheel and the Potter's nail-pierced hands? So Solomon yielded his specially hand-painted vessel for the eternal purposes of God. God delights in such prayers for Christian character, rather than the copycat Christian's cry: "Make me like someone else."

And now we come to the sad part of the story. We have to ask why it was that Solomon, who began so well, stumbled and fell so badly. Who cut in on him and hindered his progress? Who was the enemy who set out to trip him up along the way? I suppose Solomon made the commonest of all mistakes, regarding prayer. He slackened his pace. There came a time in his life when he didn't jog on. He allowed himself to take his eye off the prize and the One who waited for him at the finish line. He did not doggedly and patiently keep a single-minded goal in sight, and he became distracted by the very blessings that God bestowed upon him. Paul warned of this in the Epistle to the Hebrews when he said, "Seeing we also are compassed about with so great a cloud of witnesses, let us lay aside every weight, and the sin which doth so easily beset us, and let us run with patience the race that is set before us, Looking unto Jesus the author and finisher of our faith . . ." (12:1, 2). Jesus thought of the race in the first place, equipped us for it, and set us off. Jesus is the Trainer, too, and Jesus is there at the finishing post. Woe betide us if we do not keep our eye on Him. He is our Prize. Paul, using the athletic analogy, again reminds us that the true athlete strips for his race. The man who doesn't do that is hindered by the clothes he wears. The picture is vivid. The sins and weights that so easily beset us can hinder our progress in the race of life.

Solomon having laid aside sins and weights at the beginning of his reign, just as an athlete lays aside his outer garments, got dressed again somewhere along the way. He lost interest in the race, and began instead to be more concerned about the female spectators who were watching him.

It was this man who later in life spoke as a thoroughly disillusioned man of the world saying, "Dead flies cause the ointment of the apothecary to send forth a stinking savour: so doth a little folly him that is in reputation for wisdom and honour" (Ecclesiastes 10:1). Yes, it was Solomon who said that. If ever a man had been held in reputation for wisdom and honor, it was *this* man. If ever we doubt that, we can find verification of the fact in history, and particularly Hebrew history which tells us: "So king Solomon exceeded all the kings of the earth for riches and for wisdom. And all the earth sought to Solomon, to hear his wisdom, which God had put in his heart" (1 Kings 10:23, 24).

God made Solomon a teacher, philosopher, and preacher *par excellence.* He became a botanist and grew knowledgeable concerning metals. He composed 1,005 songs (including a golden disc called "The Song of Solomon") and wrote 3,000 proverbs! He understood the habits of animals, insects, and fish—yet the dead fly was allowed to fall into the ointment. The little foolishness fouled up the sweet savor and the ensuing smell did irreparable damage to the name of the Lord.

First Kings 11 tells us: "But King Solomon loved many foreign women; in addition to the daughter of Pharaoh, women of the Moabites, Ammonites, Edomites, Sidonians, and Hittites, of the nations concerning which the Lord said unto the children of Israel, Ye shall not go in to them, neither shall they come in unto you; for surely they will turn away your heart after their gods. Solomon clung unto these in love. And he had seven hundred wives, princesses, and three hundred concubines; and his wives turned away his heart" (*see* verses 1–3).

It's not so much how a man starts his Christian life that matters, you see. It's how he *finishes* it; just as it's really not how a man starts a race that counts, but how he ends it. At the beginning of his reign, Solomon loved the Lord and walked in the statutes of his father, David. A lifetime later we read a sad, sad statement: "Solomon did evil in the sight of the Lord, and went not fully after the Lord, as did David his father. . . . And the Lord was angry with Solomon . . ." (1 Kings 11:6, 9). What a shame, and after such a promising start. After strengthening the kingdom of Israel and building the temple of the Lord, he conceded the race. He was, in the final analysis, a hindered harrier. In the end, the bottom line is the finishing line!

What sort of a runner are you? Did you set off in grand style at a fast pace, making a great impression on the spectators around you, only to find yourself spent? Did you peak too soon? Did you forget to strip away all the sins and weights that would hinder your running? Did you quit this side of the barrier, or perhaps having done well with the point of push, run right out of the race simply because, like Solomon, you chose not to obey the truth?

Where are you? Which lap? Oh, how I pray that somehow, somewhere within the pages of this book you have been able to evaluate your position in the race. I pray, too, that you have been able to admit your failure and come to believe that failure is never, never final, whoever, wherever, *whatever* you are! Whether you be a brittle bone, gripy grape, prodigal prig, or a shaggy sheep, or at this point—a hindered harrier—I hope I have been able to show you that failure is not the end, but can be turned instead into a new beginning. A famous preacher said, "The way to up is down." It is—it really is—that is, if you decide to get up and race on, even after falling flat on your face. I pray that in the end, unlike Solomon, you will jog on and on and on—looking unto Jesus who is the Author and Finisher of your faith!

> May the mind of Christ, my Savior,
> Live in me from day to day,
> By His love and pow'r controlling
> All I do and say.
>
> May the Love of Jesus fill me,
> As the waters fill the sea;
> Him exalting, self abasing—
> This is victory.
>
> May I run the race before me,
> Strong and brave to face the foe,
> Looking only unto Jesus
> As I onward go.
>
> May His beauty rest upon me
> As I seek the lost to win,
> And may they forget the channel,
> Seeing only Him.

KATE B. WILKINSON

WORKSHEET

Hindered Harriers

EVALUATION (*This can also be used as group discussion and prayer sheet.*)

Write a sentence for each question, after reviewing the following verses:

1 Kings 3:10–14	1 Corinthians 9:24
Galatians 5:7	Philippians 3:14
Hebrews 12:1	2 Timothy 4:7

1. When did you start the race?
2. Which lap are you on?
3. What is your condition at *this* point?
4. What do the spectators see?
5. What does God see?
6. What do you see?
7. What can you learn from Solomon?
8. What do you need to pray about?
9. Prayer Time

> May I run the race before me,
> Strong and brave to face the foe,
> Looking only unto Jesus
> As I onward go.

Pray a prayer of your very own that pleases God.

Then—jog on.